FATHER'S GIFT

THREE BIG PILLARS

LT. COL. VINCE NWAFOR, US ARMY (RET.)

ARCHWAY
PUBLISHING

Archway Publishing books may be ordered through booksellers or by contacting:

Archway Publishing
1663 Liberty Drive
Bloomington, IN 47403
www.archwaypublishing.com
844-669-3957

ISBN: 978-1-6657-4058-6 (sc)
ISBN: 978-1-6657-4057-9 (hc)
ISBN: 978-1-6657-4133-0 (e)

Library of Congress Control Number: 2023905399

Print information available on the last page.

Archway Publishing rev. date: 03/27/2023

To my father, a gentle soul who saw every reason to laugh heartily. A man who left footprints to help others find their way. His earned salutation name, "Ome-mma," he who does good, says it all.

CONTENTS

Part IV: Family

Part V: At Forty, Tiger Looks Back

PREFACE

By the time you have finished this book, your imagination will be stretched, and seeds will be planted. You will be in a position to envision your golden years with minimal fumbles on life's big decisions. And your anxiety level will no longer surge when you mull over the thread of challenges tied to your anchor rope and your life journey.

Father's Gift will untwine your lifeline into the triad of self-empowerment, building wealth, and family relationships. Its story line will offer you a lens to see through during your life voyage. You will feel like you knew what was coming up and had time to plan for it. You will be able to see things instead of endlessly looking for them. You get the big decisions right; you will put order into the chaos of life. Hopefully you will hold onto the great feelings of traveling to a place you never want to forget.

You will be reminded that life is full of choices. Your decisions only take minutes to make, but their impacts could last a lifetime. If you make better choices, you can expect a better future.

You need to stay nimble to stay afloat in life. Life is not static. It is dynamic. Things around you will change, and you will change too. You do not need any extra baggage. It has a cost; it will weigh you down. Societal idiosyncrasies will be there to spar with your survival instinct, and everything is connected.

Among other points that will come alive in this book is not letting fears of life's uncertainties deter you from taking deserved risks. Former Congressman John Lewis often said, "Make good trouble." The only way to know is to try, right? And if not now, when? When the desirable is not available, the available becomes the desirable.

Father's Gift will encourage you to seize the opportunities that allow you to be what you could be and should be. You own the rights to be yourself in your own game, but you can only be one person at a time—unless you have a multiple personality disorder. As you make your bed, so shall you lie on it. Let the journey begin.

Once you have decided on your why and what, fill in the blanks with your when, where, and how. Learn what is effective, be effective, and then be efficient. Activity is not an accomplishment. Make progress. No sane person cerebrates failure.

Try to finish what you start. Halfway done is still undone. Persevere. It is darkest before the dawn. Stars only show in the dark. Right actions bring right results. Being successful feels good, and once you taste it, you will never want to fail.

Father's Gift offers you a way to break the fever of having no manual for your life journey. The help is here. Like a caterpillar transforming into a butterfly, you now have the power to write your future and a beautiful ending—yes, with minimal regrets and do-overs.

INTRODUCTION

There are some things I wish I knew earlier. Some of those things were taken for granted. Why not make them available to everyone?

Many grown-ups wish they knew what they know about life years ago. A blueprint for meandering through all the stages of life would be wonderful.

There are road maps for land navigation. There are manuals to put things together and operate things, but there is no one-size-fits-all instruction book for managing life and becoming a better life player.

Who does not want a glimpse of the future and a chance to plan ahead and bypass any roadblocks? Problem identified! Rather than finding fault and fixing blame, in my own little way, I will do something. The idea for *Father's Gift* was conceived.

Father's Gift is intended to help you find your way early in life. It will plant the seeds of hunger, help you learn and grow with the seasons of life, and improve the seeds you reap. *Father's Gift* will help you think ahead in time and space and know which direction you are moving in. It will help you look at your performance with a realistic viewpoint.

I believe in the humility of science. If you apply a known quantity in a given condition, the result will be the same. Science is validating what nature has already figured out.

An average young person does not come into the world with royal trappings, generational wealth, an inheritance, a charted life course, and high-society mentorship, but you do not have need to be jealous of anyone. If you truly make do with what you have, you will be OK.

Worry about what you want to be and what you can be. With discipline, commitment, doing your best, and taking one day at a time, your dreams will come true.

Your duty is to find your true you and discover the purpose of your life journey. Do your best every day, trust your abilities, and trust yourself.

Do not hope others will come to your rescue or rely on others; if you do, you will be disappointed when situations go sour. Even your own shadow will leave you in the dark. You must learn to be your own cheerleader.

If you fail to plan your future and work hard for it—and solely rely on God to provide—you will be disappointed when God's agenda overrides yours. You need to be proactive with your actions.

It is important that you plan and act for yourself. It is important that you know where you are and where you want to go. It is important that you know what to look for during your life journey. Your life will be partitioned into sprints and marathons. You must know when to sprint to establish your mojo and when to take on the marathons to sustain your purpose and relevancy.

Fortunately, actionable information and ideas are always around for those who are tuned in. Keep your ears open and your eyes on the lookout for the golden fleece. The future is uncertain, but if you are not focusing on something, your future might rush by while you are in a deep slumber. Search actively for the things you want, but remember that the things you want may not come to you.

Your success will require a lot of steps, and skipping any of these steps could send you into a life of futility.

The sooner you start exploring and exploiting your passions, the better. Some of these passions will reveal themselves more naturally than others will. Practicing activities in your areas of interest will reaffirm your natural gifts and affinities. Your love for certain walks of life will be transparent to you. Your successes and mistakes will be life lessons.

Stay with what gives you joy and happiness. Happiness is mostly a U-shaped curve—up, down, up. Never let the quest for perfection stymie your passions. Keep the engine running.

I was afraid my experiences would die with me if they were not written down and passed on to others. Too many people have died and perished with their knowledge unrecorded.

In William Shakespeare's *Julius Caesar*, Marc Antony rebuked the Romans after Caesar's brutal murder: "The evil that men do lives after them. The good is oft interred with their bones." While Marc Antony explicitly condemned the brutal murder, he implicitly hammered the loss of a good man, Caesar. Generations have come and passed, leaving us with little to no details about the lives they lived. If not for that, the archeologists might not have a job. We are constantly reinventing the wheel. Knowledge immortalized in print can help ensure that good people are not interred with their bones.

Why not condense my nuggets of wisdom and pass them forward? I made the choice to put in print what I did and did not do—my jambalaya of experiences or lack thereof—selected teaching points from the crucible of my trials and tribulations and put them into perpetuity. By giving it life, I can give the next generation of inquiring minds a head start. This pleases my soul. I want to help others look ahead and stop reinventing the wheel.

Providing fatherly guidance to boys and girls everywhere leaves me with a good feeling. I hope you will benefit from my luxurious look back in time. I share the things I saw, heard, felt, read, and wished I knew. This book illuminates the pathway ahead. It could give you a leg up in life. It could help you plan to succeed because failing to plan is planning to fail.

For a minute, I am humbly asking you to permit me to toot my own horn. I have been around the block a few times. I have been there and done that. In my Igbo tribe, Nigeria, we say a story is better told by the one who killed the lion. While I do not know it all, I have a firsthand account to offer. Information is power, but it has to be accurate to give you an edge. This book gives you an advance copy of life. Someday, in your life cycle, everything will make perfect sense.

I am thrilled and could not wait to give you advice from my stock of wisdom. I am not satisfied unless I am contributing something or helping others. I am filled with joy about creating something bigger than myself. In my own little way, I want the next generation to see further than I did when they think about their life cycles.

Throughout this book, I ask questions and answer them with my unique signature: diction. This montage of prose reflects my African roots and my life in America, my adopted home country. I have codified my advice in print to reach people far and wide because success with successors is true success—and success without successors is the end of the story. At the least, I am giving something to others. I am happy to pass the baton, but you might not be as good as the original. Ha, ha, ha!

The past is not the future, and tomorrow is longer than yesterday. You cannot learn everything in one book. No single book tells the entire story. You have to read a lot more, and you have to read voraciously. Ultimately, you will grow from your own experiences.

Father's Gift is not a Band-Aid or a quick fix. It is intended to have a positive, lasting influence on the elements of your life cycle.

An identified problem is a half-solved problem. Risks need to be addressed up front. Endlessly dwelling on your misfortunes does no good. Instead, control what you get into in life and positively engage yourself.

You now have the playbook. Learn the plays, practice them, and ask others for help as required.

I appreciate you partaking in my labor of love. If I inspire you to make better choices and avoid do-overs in life, we have both won. You refresh yourself; you refresh me. Let the countdown begin.

My Messaging Style

In the long run, most people remember stories better than straight lists of facts. As a result, I have condensed my story into teachable moments. It will lend a voice to my life field report, which would otherwise get lost in the echo chamber of nothingness. My knowledge would be gone forever.

I have published six articles in professional military magazines, but this is my first book. I have always thought about writing a book like my namesake, Vincent Chukwuemeka Ike, my hometown king, the late Eze Ikelionwu XI of an Aro town, Ndikelionwu, Anambra state, Nigeria. He was one of the most renowned Nigerian novelists, and he has more books to his credit than can be counted on my fingers. Also, my village produced another great author, an elder and honorable statesman, Peter Nwankwo, principal partner of P. C. Nwankwo & Co. Estate Surveyors and Valuers. Elder Peter Nwankwo has published four books. The works of my hometown's authors inspired me to become an author. I know I will make my people and my ancestors proud.

Ndikelionwu means people from the stock of warriors who defied death. Back in the olden days, in centuries past, when men where men who strangled wild animals with their bare hands, Ndikelionwu was revered. The mere invocation of her name struck fear in the hearts of mortals, particularly would-be adversaries. Also, records show that Ndikelionwu was the cradle of Christianity to many communities. Why did the early European missionaries try to convert Ndikelionwu? Go figure—your guess is as good as mine!

Colloquial speaking that appears spontaneous and spunky impresses me. I appreciate wordplay and word power as in figures of speech. Recognizing the intellectual ability it takes to string words together is soothing to my soul. I have a penchant for alliteration (repetition of beginning sounds), anaphora (phrases that begin with the same word), metaphor (comparing two unlike things), irony (contrast between what is said and reality), simile (comparison of two unlike things using like), assonance (repetition of vowel sounds), hyperbole (exaggeration for effect), proverb (nonliteral expression perceived as truth), idiom (a group of words with peculiar meaning, which to a layperson is unpredictable from the meaning of each individual word), and riddles.

My flair for proverbs, idioms, and riddles comes naturally. As a son of the Igbo tribe, my native tongue is Igbo, a language in which proverbs, idioms, and riddles spar with the essence of the message.

Igbos use proverbs, idioms, and riddles interchangeably to convey the gist of a story. I can barely tell the differences between them. I see riddles as enigmas finely wrapped in common words to spice up conversations and inform the wise while leaving the fool out to dry. We use riddles to drive home important messages. The way the speakers employ and deploy riddles speaks to their wit, wisdom, and intellectual sharpness. Dry and satirical humor is normal. Many Igbo conversations have the vibe of a Dave Chappelle comedy show.

I am a proud product of African and American cultures. I would be remiss if I failed to give a shout-out from the rooftop: America is super welcoming. America gave me the freedom and liberty to use my God-given gifts. This is such a blessing and an amalgamation of both worlds, including writing styles.

I am glad I have the knife and the yam in my hand; it is my honor to cut the yam as I see fit. I intend to express and impress upon you that you can learn from me and turn out better than I did. Join me as I tell you what I will tell you—and tell you—and tell you what I told you.

Expect the salient themes to be stressed in different ways to drive home the points and put order to life's chaos. In the end, the topics that appear to be independent at first will be interdependent.

PART I

TIGER

Jena and Johnny had three kids: Tiger, Charlie, and Eva. Part I explains the kids' upbringing and the onset of the impactful role of the kids' maternal grandpa, George (GG), in their lives.

CHAPTER 1

TIGER ARRIVED

Six months after Jena's wedding, she announced to her family at the Thanksgiving Day gathering, "We are expecting a baby boy."

Her mother, Anna, was the happiest she had ever been because she wanted to be a grandmother so badly. Jena's father, George, was thrilled. He could not wait to teach his grandchild life's lessons.

Jena's brother, Monty, was very pleased his sister was about to realize her dream of becoming a mother with Johnny, the man she loved so much and married.

The feelings of Rita, Jena's older sister, about her younger sister's pregnancy were lukewarm at best. Rita's only son, Hawk, was excited he would soon have a cousin.

Johnny's sister, Viola, had taken a liking to Jena ever since she had married into their family, and they had become tight friends. Viola welcomed the news her nephew was on his way.

In some form or another, these relatives would impact the life of Jena and Johnny's baby. In addition to the family members, other people would shape the baby's life: schoolteachers, classmates, neighbors, friends, and public figures. The actions of people in government, sports, and entertainment would contribute to shaping who the baby would turn out to be. If the baby was lucky enough to have siblings—sisters and/or brothers—they would also be part of the equation.

Jena's baby would not be born with silver spoon in his mouth—more like a plastic spoon. Jena and Johnny were a working family. They put their talents to work and succeeded as a two-income household.

Both husband and wife have great physical characteristics. Johnny was five foot eleven and had a muscular frame. Jena was five foot eight, and she was built like a model.

Jena and Johnny believed in personal responsibility. The couple's values were based on their belief in the Word of God, the Bible, which made sense because the quickest way to be courageous and fearless is to believe in God. They prayed their baby would be all they were and more.

Like many parents, the couple had many plans and expectations for their baby. They thought about welcoming the baby home. They thought about raising the child and the world the child would live in. They had mixed feelings, both happiness and stress, because the baby's life journey was uncharted.

Given Jena and Johnny's many worries about the challenges their firstborn would face on his life journey, it is hard to believe that the family welcomed their second and third children within three short years after Tiger's birth.

CHAPTER 2

GROWING UP

As the oldest, Tiger was a role model by default for Charlie, his younger brother, and Eva, his only sister. No one gave Tiger the job description, but it came naturally. (Really? Not so fast. Tiger learned to play the role more by trial and error.)

When Charlie was born, Tiger was only fifteen months old, and he was three years old when Eva came along. Although Tiger could not pick up his siblings as babies, he often clasped them, sharing his love and brotherly warmth. When the babies burped, Tiger always said, "Yup," and he showed them his glimmering face. When they smiled, Tiger returned the favor, softly touching their cheeks and making gibberish baby sounds. Amazingly, his sounds and smiles were reciprocated. It seemed like they somehow understood each other's intentions.

Mom Jena and Daddy Johnny, Tiger's parents, were usually a few feet away, watching happily and imagining what Tiger, Charlie, and Eva would become. Mom Jena and Daddy Johnny wanted the best for their children. It came naturally too. (Really? Not so fast. Young and new parents do not have all the answers. They fly by the seat of their pants.)

As good parents, they showed unconditional love; they positively inspired and influenced their children to be better than they were. Do not fool yourself: unconditional love does not mean zero conditions. Parents tacitly hold some conditions—to be good and successful or to be bad and a black eye to the family.

Luckily for Jena and Johnny, Grandpa George (GG) and Grandma Ann (Gma), their kids' maternal grandparents, provided a connecting bridge: what the past was, what the present is, and what the future could be.

Very early in their children's lives, Jena and Johnny found an oasis of information to expand and satisfy their kids' intellectual curiosity and capacity. They inspired a hunger in their children to achieve their life purpose. They were their kids' sounding boards, guides, and support systems. Jena and Johnny followed the "do what we do and not just as we say" model. They accepted their weaknesses and worked on them. They showed kindness and honesty in what they did.

When Tiger, Charlie, and Eva saw that their parents were doing their best, they said their parents were the best in the whole world—a priceless compliment from kids to their parents.

Good Times

Tiger remembered the good times he had with Charlie and Eva early in their lives. The family ate together at their dining table, along with GG and Gma. Stories and lessons about eating etiquette were part of each meal. Do not talk with food in your mouth. Chew slow. Eat with your right hand. Keep to your own plate. Cover your mouth when you cough or yawn. Eat with a fork. Use the knife with your left hand. Take your plate to the kitchen when you are done. This guidance contributed to who and what Tiger would become.

Mom Jena dressed her kids in coordinated colors to show they were siblings. From the time he was a toddler, Charlie wore hand-me-down clothes from Tiger, and he resented that Tiger mostly had new clothes. Tiger's memory remained fresh of the day their mother gave Charlie a good spanking and put him in a time-out for hitting his brother's head with a teacup when he bickered about Tiger's new clothes.

Playing hide-and-seek was among the siblings' pastimes. They also liked to run around and wrestle in their backyard with Daddy Johnny and occasionally GG. Tiger was very happy when he beat his daddy in a sprint. Daddy Johnny conceded. He gracefully blamed it on getting old and took a moment to reflect on how fast he used to run. For Tiger, outsprinting his daddy reaffirmed him as grown. He was a big boy.

Mom Jena made sure books of different genres were available for the kids to read. She got most of the books for a few dollars from used bookstores or Salvation Army stores. Newer books were borrowed from the local public library. On family nights, the kids told stories from the books they read.

Serving as a stabilizing force, Mom Jena and Daddy Johnny extrapolated from their kids' interests and joked about the different vocations they would desire their kids to embark on for life. The kids enjoyed the exchange of stories and social time. Mom Jena and Daddy Johnny guided their kids while allowing their unformed, inquisitive minds to blossom.

Before each of the kids turned six, they were indoctrinated into the habit of reading books in a lifelong quest for knowledge. Knowledge is the power Mom Jena and Daddy Johnny gave to their kids.

By fourteen years of age, Charlie was as tall as Tiger. The duo was very athletic and played on their school's sports teams. Tiger was into football and wrestling. In track and field, he took part in hundred-meter track events and shot put. In addition to playing soccer, Charlie followed his brother's footsteps and basked in the name recognition made by Tiger. Eva was on the track and basketball teams, and she made her own name.

Between their athletic events, Mom Jena squeezed in piano lessons to expose them to music appreciation. The kids also participated in scouting. There was no denying the siblings' life lessons on teamwork, and their competitive spirit grew richer.

Mom Jena earned the title of "Supermom" for taking the kids to all those extracurricular activities and bringing refreshments for their teams. Tiger would never forget his mother's sacrifices.

In high school, not too many people messed with the siblings. They all had each other's backs. Tiger and Charlie were very defensive of Eva, their younger and only sister.

Their friends ran in the same circles. Bonfire nights at their house drew the most popular kids in the neighborhood. They had potluck snacks, hot dogs, marshmallows, and sodas. All the kids took pride in keeping the bonfire ablaze. They collected dry shrubs from around the neighborhood to keep the fire going. From dusk to late at night, the kids crackled with laughter and made jokes at one another's expense. They roasted hot dogs and marshmallows on sticks. As the bonfire and night wore down, a pizza delivery followed. More eating.

They also played fun games like rock paper scissors. They enjoyed it because nobody dominated. A different player emerged as champion at the end of each set. Tiger's best friend, Tony, was always the life of the party. As the night wore down, a few of their friends might end up sleeping over.

Mom Jena and Daddy Johnny reluctantly learned to tolerate and accept the crowd and their antics: hanging out, making s'mores, eating hot dogs, and wild, high-pitched laughs. And they would talk into the wee hours of the morning.

A Bullying Incident

Bolton tormented his classmates. Because Tiger and Tony spoke up for others against Bolton's bullying, they had to enter the eye of the storm. Bolton unleashed his wrath on them.

One day, Tiger was fed up with the bullying and challenged Bolton to a no-holds-barred fight after school. Bolton mocked Tiger and boisterously accepted the challenge. At the appointed hour, Bolton wasted no time in getting Tiger into a choke hold—but Tiger stomped on Bolton's right toe, jerked to the left, and broke free.

Both fighters were surrounded and watched by their jeering and cheering classmates. Of course, many of the classmates rooted for Tiger. They were very happy that someone was standing up against the bully.

By the second minutes of the fight, Bolton had the upper hand again. He wrestled Tiger down, and the classmates' cheers abruptly stopped.

Tiger did not stay pinned down for long. He drew gas from his reserve tank, mustered his energy, tucked his left leg toward his buttocks, flipped himself over the bully for a moment, and jumped off Bolton. His classmates cheered again.

Bolton got up, and he was angrier than ever. He swooped down to pull Tiger by the legs.

Tiger lobbed a counter right hook jab that connected fully to Bolton's left neck-jaw region and knocked him out cold.

Bolton fell backward, landed on the ground, and went limp. The classmates' roaring cheers quickly gave way to somber cries that Tiger had killed Bolton.

Before the emergency medical help could arrive to resuscitate Bolton, he got up on his own. Feebly, Bolton walked away with his head down.

From that minute on, Bolton's bullying became history. It took a long time for Bolton to get back in his classmates' good graces.

Tiger walked off taller, and he gained fame for putting Bolton in his place. Therefore, never bow down to a bully. You will never beat a bully by turning the other cheek. Stand your ground.

Tiger reported the bully and the situation to his teacher, Mom Jena, and Daddy Johnny. Stand your ground and fight back against the bully.

Tiger was a Good Samaritan. He cared about what would have happened if he failed to speak up. If you see something, you should say something. Do not let inaction consume your conscience. You must continue doing the right things the right way.

Ride a Bicycle

Tiger wanted to learn to ride a bicycle and a motorcycle. The freedom and liberation of riding a bike cannot be overstated. Beginners struggle to keep their bicycles upright and pedal at the same time. Falling off a bike is common too—and so was sustaining bruises on knees and elbows. Sometimes knuckles get bruised too. The key is perseverance. Tiger tried, failed, and tried again until he succeeded. Tiger learned to ride his bike within a month.

Daddy Johnny held the bike while Tiger mounted it. Next, Tiger tried pedaling. The bike was wobbly and unsteady, but it stayed upright because of Daddy Johnny's anchoring support. Once Tiger got stronger with the pedaling and was able to sustain the effort, the forward motion overcame gravity and prevented the bike from falling.

Daddy Johnny's encouragement to Tiger was priceless. Daddy Johnny praised any progress Tiger made. That was the first time

Tiger confronted his fears and nurtured his warrior spirit. Tiger had conquered his desperation with perseverance.

The first time Tiger rode solo without Daddy Johnny's assistance, he felt like he was in control. He was on top of the world.

Tiger's siblings learned to ride too. Riding happily with family and friends were memorable moments in the siblings' young lives.

Years after learning how to ride a bike, Tiger wanted to learn to ride a motorcycle. While many people can say they have ridden a bike, not as many can say they have ridden a motorcycle.

Tiger borrowed a motorcycle from his best friend. Tiger surprised himself when he was able to mount and ride the motorcycle after some instructions from Tony: "Hold down the clutch, engage the gear, and release slowly while you accelerate the throttle. To stop, clutch down and brake."

It was so much fun. Tiger's first ride was flawless and pure fun.

Tiger enjoyed riding the borrowed motorcycle until the fateful day he took it without Tony's permission. He found out, as far as motorcycles were concerned, he had a long way to go to be savvy about the rules of the road. Tiger sped up, weaving in and out of traffic, and fell off the motorcycle when he failed to properly negotiate a sharp corner. Tiger suffered road rash after his pants were shredded by the paved road. He was not wearing proper protective equipment. The motorcycle sustained some minor damage.

Afraid and disappointed, Tiger rolled the motorcycle back and parked it without telling Tony what had happened. A day passed before Tony noticed his wrecked motorcycle. Tony knew immediately that Tiger was the only person who could have done it. Needless to say, Tony was so mad that he could have cut Tiger's legs off.

Tony and Tiger were weighed down by the burden of telling their parents about the motorcycle accident, but they did. Tony's parents thanked God Tiger was OK, and they got the motorcycle repaired. Tiger's parents surprised him. After they chastised Tiger for taking Tony's motorcycle without permission, they promised to get him a pre-owned motorcycle.

Tiger got his own motorcycle, and over time, he mastered defensive driving. He learned to always drive below the speed limit, look out for what the cars around him were doing, make himself visible, and avoid other vehicles' blind spots.

The adrenaline rush from riding the motorcycle was so different than with the bicycle. Being in rapid motion was thrilling. Focusing on distances, paths, and plans to negotiate the paths kept him on edge. Traffic jams had less of an impact on motorcycles than other vehicles. He could whizz in, out, and around the traffic.

Overdoing anything is bad. Falling off a fast-moving motorcycle is unforgivable. The air whizzing past his face was exhalating and intoxicating. He felt the rider's high, but he had to watch his speed. Everyone should ride a motorcycle at least a few times.

◆　◆　◆

Tiger's encounter with a street magician remains fresh in his memory too.

The magician's quick sleight of hand as he entertained and manipulated three cards was a learning point for Tiger. All three cards were facing down. The king of spades was the winning card. The diamond card and the club card were decoys. Following the magician's quick sleight of hand, spectators—untrained eyes like Tiger—often thought they had hunch about which card was the winning card until they faced off with the street magician.

Picking the correct card would double their wager. The street magicians planted and connived with their compatriots by flipping the cards and hiding the winning card. The winning streaks of the planted magicians would often prod and lure spectators into a false sense of security and a fierce urge to make some quick, easy money.

Tiger was no exception. He took the street magician's bait and came out on the short end of the stick. He left empty-handed. Tiger lost everything—one-hundred dollars—which he had saved up for his college application fees.

Tiger's first twenty dollars vanished when he picked the decoy card. His second twenty dollars went down like the first. Tiger was infatuated, hooked, and desperate. He was about to bet the sixty dollars left in his pocket, believing he could win back his lost money—with something extra. Tony sensed Tiger's plight, grabbed Tiger's collar, and pulled him out of the betting pit.

Tiger pushed Tony away and returned to the betting pit to play his last sixty dollars.

Tony had never seen Tiger's unruly side and immediately left the scene.

After Tiger's first and second bets went down the drain, his third and final bet was no different. Tiger cried and asked the street magician to return his wagers, but it fell on deaf ears. The street magicians laughed at him, folded up quickly, and scurried away. The spectators dispersed too. Tiger was standing alone with tears running down his cheeks.

The tears were about the loss of his entire savings, for not listening to Tony, and for being greedy. He had been angling for a get-rich-quick scheme that never happened. Lastly, what would Daddy Johnny and Mom Jena do when they heard the news?

The urge for easy money had blinded Tiger's critical judgment: whether to wage a bet, how much to wage, and when to quit and walk away. Tiger swore never to pay attention to another get-rich-quick scheme.

◆ ◆ ◆

One more thing remaining fresh in Tiger's mind was his peers believing he was naturally intelligent. Tiger never considered himself a super gifted student, but many of his peers thought otherwise. In Tiger's mind, if it were not for *Father's Gift*, the book his maternal grandpa (GG) wrote as a walking stick for the madness of life, Tiger would be a different person. Tiger believed he was just hardworking and had been given the right tools to be better than average.

From the beginning, Tiger knew what counted was not the hours you put in; it was what you put into those hours. You need to be there—where you are. No precedent does not mean you cannot make a precedent. Be careful because you can make little or big errors in both directions on the stairs of life.

By design, GG boiled down nine elements (personal hygiene, character building, education, learning, belief in God, health, leadership, public speaking, and politics) into a gateway to self-empowerment. GG says if you are self-empowered, the sky is your limit.

As soon as Tiger could read, on his sixth birthday, GG gave him a lifelong gift. It was not money; it was knowledge. *Father's Gift*, detailing GG's nuggets of wisdom and his life experiments—would make his grandson's life journey less chaotic. GG gave Tiger a tool for self-empowerment, building wealth, and family relationship. Lucky Tiger.

Tiger attributed his book smarts to Mom Jena, and her role in making her kids book smart cannot be overstressed. Mom Jena got Tiger to invest his raw energy in learning very early in life. Mom Jena taught her kids the alphabets and numbers up to one hundred as soon as they could talk, which was no later than age four. She got them to sing the alphabet in songs, which earlier generations did. There was no reinventing the wheel. She made learning fun—by singing it.

Learning to count with fingers and toes excited the kids. After learning the first twenty numbers, Mom Jena added tens— like thirty, forty, and fifty—up to one hundred. Then, she filled in the in-between numbers. She got the kids to memorize the sequences by repeating them over and over during the day, before they went to sleep, and immediately after they woke up. Slowly and gradually, the information sank into the kids' subconscious minds, and they could recite them effortlessly.

The next stage in Mom Jena's teaching her kids was identifying and writing the letters and numbers they had learned to vocalize. She followed a similar learning sequence as in the earlier stages. They practiced, practiced, and practiced until the kids got it.

The third stage was applying the letters and numbers as lifelong learning building blocks. Early reading ability and simple arithmetic ability did wonders for the children. Audio comes first, and visual comes second.

Mom Jena said it, and the kids repeated it over and over until it sank in. She showed them artwork until the kids could masterly identify them.

For reading, Mom Jena started her kids with learning one syllable, followed by two syllables, and then three syllables. They practiced and practiced. They strung the syllables together and said the words. Eventually, the kids were able to string the words together and read sentences. Welcome. The magic door of reading had swung open.

For simple arithmetic, addition and subtraction were a great starting point. Finger counting worked to internalize the concepts. Using coins and visual objects to learn the numbers after ten was critical.

Once addition and subtraction principles were rooted in her kids' brains, Mom Jena moved on to teaching multiplication.

Mom Jena made the kids say and memorize multiplication table sets up to twelve times twelve.

The right time to introduce the division concept was when the kids could correctly answer every question on the multiplication table. Even-number division tended to be easier for beginners until they could conceptualize the step-by-step process.

Mom Jena knew patience was a virtue when teaching the early building blocks of knowledge. She continued the practice and expanded her kids' reading and arithmetic assignments.

Daddy Johnny's daily guidance and Mom Jena's motherly care with *Father's Gift* were the reasons her kids developed a fondness for learning. They were hungry for knowledge.

Tiger used *Father's Gift* like a walking stick in the dark. From an early age, Tiger knew the value of self-empowerment, building wealth, and strong family relationships. *Father's Gift* influenced who Tiger turned out to be, and it gave him the confidence to face the world.

As far as Tiger was concerned, the teaching points in *Father's Gift* are worthy of recitation for posterity.

PART II

SELF-EMPOWERMENT

GG's first pillar of life is self-empowerment. Because charity begins at home, getting your house in order should be the top priority. Personal hygiene is the first order of business, and character is next. Your character is your foundation, and you cannot afford to be skimpy with it. You need structured education early in life. The cornerstone of lifelong learning will fuel your general knowledge. Belief in God, moral well-being, and spiritual well-being are also part of the equation. Your health—your most coveted possession—deserves your undivided attention. You need solid leadership skills to obtain results with others. Be prepared for public speaking if you are going to represent others or communicate with groups of people. As political animals, everyone in modern society, including you, has politics on the menu. If you are in tune with these elements, you will be self-empowered.

CHAPTER 3

PERSONAL HYGIENE

To prevent dragon breath, GG recommends starting the day with mouth hygiene. In the morning, attack your oral hygiene. Floss to remove food lodged in between the teeth. Wet your toothbrush and apply about half an inch of toothpaste to it. Not all toothpastes are the same. The best ones fight plaque, prevent cavities, have teeth-whitening agents, and get rid of bad breath. Brush your teeth using a soft-bristle toothbrush in gentle and circular motion. Swirl and brush front teeth, side teeth, teeth surface, and behind teeth. Replace your toothbrush every four months. Do not forget to scrub your tongue with a spatula-like object to remove the gooey stuff. Rinse your mouth with mouthwash.

After the afternoon meal, repeat the teeth-cleaning routine. You may abbreviate the process this time. At bedtime, repeat the full-course routine. For fresh breath, brush your teeth two or three times daily.

Take a bath in the morning to refresh yourself for the day ahead. Use good body wash or soap. Wash the body, armpits, groin area, legs, and head. Immediately after the bath or shower, apply high-quality deodorant to the armpits, massage the body with moisturizing lotion, and apply anti-chap ointment to the lips. Once your body is prepped, put on clean underwear, undershirt, and socks as desired.

Wear hip brief underwear for slim-cut fitting and better support or boxer brief (snug and extend to thigh) for an active lifestyle. Standard boxers are loose and allow cooler temperatures in the groin area. Standard boxers are best worn around the house.

Silk and cotton materials make for comfortable underwear. They are breathable and reduce moisture in the groin. Be aware of the alternative; synthetic fabric underwear tends to trap heat and moisture, which increases the chance of bacteria breeding and skin irritation.

It is not classy for your underwear to rise above your pants. Wear a belt to keep your pants up, and do not go commando. It is impolite for a man not to wear underwear in public; it offends people. Body-touching clothes like underwear are best worn once and then put in the laundry basket.

At night, at home, dress in very loose clothes after your shower. Pamper your body with feel-good, soothing aromatherapy body care lotion to prepare for sleep. You will fall into a deep slumber—hopefully on a trip to wonderland. Dress appropriately for the day.

Be cognizant about what you wear. Color coordination makes a statement about you, shows your personality, and says a lot about you.

When you have a job, clothes make a man. This is no lie. Dress and play the part. First impressions count.

When you think about clothes, think about fitting your body type. Pick the fits and styles that make you glow. Dress in a manner that fits the times and know when to project a youthful attitude or maturity. It never hurts for a man to look his best.

Inexpensive clothes that fit perfectly will command positive attention. Someone in ill-fitted top designer and expensive clothes may not receive approving remarks. Fit and style matter the most. There is no reason to be stuck in clothes rut. Very old clothes can earn you notoriety.

You may dress stylishly in conservative clothes with just a few color combinations that match. Being conservatively trendy means knowing when classic jeans are out and when slim jeans are in. Large-collared shirts are out, and narrower cuts are in.

Solid colors look best for most clothes. Two colors that match look good too. Dressing in more than three colors can earn you a clownish look, but it all depends.

Bright colors reflect sunlight from late spring to early fall. Darker clothes absorb and retain more heat during cold seasons. Follow the flock.

Your shoes can make a statement. Three to seven pairs per season will do.

Put your clothes and shoes together and take pride in representing yourself.

Don't pay full price for clothes or accessories. Look for deals and off-season markdowns.

In general, keep all your clothing clean. Keep dirty clothes in a laundry basket and not on the floor. No one should have to pick up your dirty clothes. Wash any dirty clothes at least once per week. Wearing the same clothes twice will not feel fresh. Do not forget about alternating shoes every other day to air them out and prevent fungus growth, fungus toes, and foot odor.

Good personal hygiene and clean clothes will build your confidence and make you feel good.

Personal grooming must not be left at the back burner during puberty and beyond. Puberty in boys begins around fourteen. Of course, this is not a hard-and-fast rule. Each person grows at his own pace. However, between eighteen and twenty-one, boys appear to be fully grown. Along with the physical growth comes interest in the opposite sex, acne, facial hair, pubic hair, and body odor. The name of the game is being neat and tidy.

A few pimples here and there seem to be a rite of passage during puberty. If you can, do some facial cleansing at night. Also, watch out for oily foods. Do not be overly worried; as you age, the acne will subside and will no longer be an issue.

Style your hair to conform with the personality you want to portray. Wearing a beard or being clean-shaven are both OK. Shaving daily with a sharp blade will help you avoid shaving bumps and will keep your face smooth. Shaving or trimming your underarms and other unwanted hairs should be routine activities.

Nothing triggers social embarrassment like body odor. Do not be a skunk. It takes time to find the right antiperspirant and deodorant for underarm care. You may be interested in the scent, but it is more important to get one that offers long-lasting sweat and odor protection. Avoid deodorants that cause irritation or leave white residue on clothes. The best time to apply deodorant is immediately after a shower and before vigorous activities.

Take care of your fingernails and toenails. Clean-cut nails are manly. Upgrade your hygiene if you constantly observe dirt under your nails. Look sharp, look and smell clean, and dress for success.

Your parents will be there to guide you through confusing times, but you can tell them if you are having difficulties. Your parents are not mind readers, and you should not expect them to telepathically know what is on your mind. Learn to say, "I need help." Your parents will do their best to get you what you need. Count on your mother to go out of her way to see you look clean, smell good, and be happy.

CHAPTER 4

CHARACTER BUILDING

According to GG, your attitude and character say it all about you—and they deserve all the attention in the world. The day you were born is your starting line, and the day you kick the bucket is your finish line. Within this window, you will go through the ups and downs of life. In between, you will build your character.

Your character may be yours, but it is not yours to abuse. If it goes awry, there will be a price to pay. If you want to have solid character, you need to get your values right, manage your life troubles, and hang around the right people.

Values

There is no all-inclusive list of values for you to know, but it pays to expand the breadth and depth of the values you know and hold. The value lessons discussed here are intentionally shared in random order to stimulate and reinforce the message.

Live your values with a sense of duty because your values represent your character. Your values will provide the hinges that hold your character in place. Your life choices and actions will depend upon the values you hold. The earlier in life you become aware of the values you hold, the better you can identify who you are. This is your character. As soon as you can, seek your purpose in life. Your values will guide you like the North Star guiding the biblical three magi visiting the birthplace of Jesus Christ in Bethlehem.

Pay attention to that little voice inside you. The gyroscope to your true north takes guidance from the values you hold. Just as a diamond in the ground is not valued until it is mined and processed, your values will remain latent until you make a choice or take action. Your values lay dormant until activated, but they affect your relationship with everything in your orbit.

When you are grounded in solid values, your character will be on autopilot—and it will be exemplary. To nurture and harness great values, begin with valuing others and seeing the value of things beyond how they look on the surface. The more you empathize, the more you will see and hear.

Appreciate the order and composition of what you see. The values you acquire will open your eyes to the method in the madness and the madness in the method. Appreciate grand theories and abstract assertions for what they are. Birds sing in the early morning to welcome the new day. The sun rises and sets to signal the passage of time. Dusk is when the world goes to sleep. Give meaning and order to the things around you. Give them due appreciation and love.

Amid the noise and haste of life, be happy that you are part of the universe. Do not forget the world does not belong to you. It is the other way around; you belong to the world. Are you being a good guest? Are you lacking in social grace? Do you live and let live? Do not wait until the eleventh hour to suddenly get religious.

Look under your feet for the rough form of a diamond; it might look like a semitransparent rock because you have an uneducated eye. Pick it up, have it cut, and polish it. What do you have? A natural diamond—and you could have missed it.

Do your part to hand a better world to the generation behind you. Everything you know about your life could change forever in the blink of an eye. You could lose a loved one or a limb. Life and death go together. Some things come sooner than you hope they will. Begin living a life you will be at peace with.

From time to time, question your values. As times change, your values might change. Do not let your values get stuck in rut. If they do, it will be like a huge stick in your bike's wheels. They will damage your bike and force you to fly off the handle to greet the ground with your forehead.

Many people will applaud traditions as good, but many others believe traditions are not good, particularly looking at them through the lens of today's perspectives. Values are no different. Your values need to be in lockstep with the times. Do not be a laggard who holds onto archaic values. Instead, be a maverick who skates to where the "values puck" is going to land.

There are choices in life, and you have the power to choose. Every situation you encounter will have two sides: positive and negative. You can choose to see the glass as half full or half empty. You can look into the night sky and be mesmerized by the astronomical arrangements of the moon and stars—or you can choose to focus on the darkness. The values you hold will help you focus on the right stuff and not the wrong stuff. Your values will help you make appropriate choices.

To achieve your objectives, borrow an idea from one of the United States Army's planning precepts. PACE stands for primary, alternate, contingency, and emergency. PACE is a multi-graduated plan with variables that are tweaked to take on a mission. Decision points in the plans offer essential trigger points. PACE plans ought to minimize all-out surprises as events unfold. The key is being prepared to adjust and adapt quickly. The right plan will take you closer to your goal, and the wrong plan will take you farther away from achieving your objective.

Take more risks as a young man. Make your hay while the sun shines. Launch trial balloons if you desire so. The world is your oyster—go get the pearls. Take good risks that are aligned with your abilities and passions.

Do your risk analysis, identify hazards and mitigations, and determine your maximum acceptable risk level before taking on a project or venture. Prepare for the worst—but expect the best. Think ahead in time and space in what you say and do. Tackle today's problem before it becomes tomorrow's crises—and get better doing them.

Progress always involves some risk, but risk should not mean staring down the barrel. You should not be too far away from the forest to see the trees.

It may be soothing to know that many of the things you worry about will never happen. So, dream big. Great ships sail in deep waters. Take on a marquee name and try to live up to the name. Make your mark. Over time, you will be an icon to be reckoned with.

You may have to run through the rain and mud to get to the main target. If you cannot get to your target because it is a bridge too far, move on to the secondary objective. If you have gone beyond the point of no return and feel lost, seek fresh ideas from others to rescue your situation. Nothing is final until it is final. Until you quit or die, do not give up on yourself.

Quitting as soon as you sense discomfort will cost you more than time; your psyche may suffer confidence deficiency. Unless you are among the few born with silver spoons in their mouths, life is not a walk in the park. Buckle up for the ride.

In your life journey, be prepared to entertain failures and rejections. You will need and want things you cannot afford. Such is life. Try to improve your stake while you make do with what you have. If horses were wishes, beggars would ride. Be real.

Understand the importance of what you do with what you have. Do not languish on what you should have had. Worrying why you were not born richer, taller, smarter, or better endowed than other people is lunacy. You come to Mother Earth as you are. Make the best of it and be the best you. Your values serve as the bedrock to how you see and feel things; they are extensions of your actions.

Whatever you believe, particularly if you do what you believe, will strongly shape your reality. Sadly, if your beliefs are false, they will be true for you. You will end up expending the few arrows in your quiver on the fallacy. What about that?

You are part of all you have being through. You are a living magnet, and you are drawn to the things you believe and think about. Your thoughts are in constant motion, triggering how you act, your habits, your character, and ultimately your destiny.

Strangely, your thoughts can take on a life of their own. Everyone is flawed in some form or another. Try to keep your strange thoughts in check. Try to be more positive, purposeful, and self-directed to do the right things right.

Absolute is an oddity if blood flows through your veins. Mistakes make you human. Even the best of us foul up sometimes. Strive for excellence—not perfection. Chasing perfection will keep you in perpetual state of dissatisfaction.

You are made on purpose for a purpose. You are special and most qualified to be you. The easiest thing to be in this world is you. If you are a soldier, aim to become a general. If you are a teacher, aim to be a principal or a superintendent. If you are a priest, aim to become the pope. If you are a journalist, strive to be the editor or the primetime news anchor of a major news network. As an entrepreneur, own multiples businesses. As a performer of any sort, become the GOAT (greatest of all time) in your line of work.

Life is short. Dream big and aim high. Do not permit anyone to tell you that you are not good enough to achieve your ambitions. Do not build obstacles to your imaginations or handicap yourself. Some challenges are natural, and some are created by you. Respect nature. Never let the difficulties of a few bad days overshadow the joy of your many good days.

Do not be unduly scared of snakes or anything else. A lot of living things are scared of you too. Be cautious and respectful when you encroach other living things' boundaries.

Believe your best version is yet to come. On a bad day, no matter how you feel, pull yourself up, buckle up, and be present. Find a positive meaning in your situation and live in the moment. This can be easier said than done, but successful people persevere. When the situation is in your rearview mirror, you will see the lessons of that moment.

Do you know your calling or destiny? Where there is no vision, people perish. Start with allowing your imagination to fly from what you are to what you could be. The sky is no longer the limit. Astronauts now live in outer space, interplanetary tourism is now a reality, and parents can now welcome their babies via surrogate mothers.

Opportunity is not money. Opportunity is a chance to explore and become who you ought to be. Opportunity allows you to try different keys on the ring until you open the door. Opportunity allows you to sight your gun on the big game. Opportunity provides you the freedom, time, and space to start. Put one foot in front of the other to find your seat in the theater of life. Opportunity allows you to find your dream and light the fuse. Opportunity makes you enthusiastic about living.

Do not just grow where you are planted; you may have to get out of your comfort zone to find opportunity. If opportunities do not find you, you should go find opportunities. Live life mostly on offense. Opportunities are not always written in the sky for you to see; you may have to peel back a couple of layers before they become transparent.

Do not let your fear of failure make you miss an opportunity. Failure is part of success. Learn from your success as well as your mistakes.

Hindsight is not twenty-twenty because people forget—and memories fade. No one is perfect except for Jesus Christ. He rose from the dead after three days. Forgive yourself for your imperfections.

Find your purpose, make your mark in life, and improve things or invent things. Be thankful for what you have and not sorry for what you do not have.

Are you the type that underrate or overrate what you don't have? Drop it. Appreciate and enjoy what you have.

Be patient. When you are by the fireside, you do not warm your hand by putting your hand inside the fire. No. Just give yourself a few minutes; sitting by the fireside will warm your blood.

Every time a banana leaves the bunch, it gets peeled and eaten. If you chase two rabbits, your attention will be divided, allowing both rabbits the chance to escape. Take life in stride.

Avoid emotional shopping sprees. Shop wisely for what you need or want. Spending money on the wrong stuff matters. At eighteen, if you are buying expensive shoes or clothes to impress others, you are heading toward the wrong side of traffic. Spend your modest means on tutorials, educational tools, technological aids, learning or entertainment trips, museums, and industrial and historical sites. That kind of stuff will enrich your learning power and knowledge.

Avoid teen pregnancy. Do not become a teenage father. If it happens, do not be an absent father. If you do, you will force your child to be one of the many at-risk kids out there.

It is not right for you to subject your kid to being raised by a single mother or another family member because you elected to be a deadbeat father or shirk your fatherly responsibilities for whatever the reasons. Your child needs you more in the early formative years. The puny, sporadic help to take care of your kid at your convenience is definitely not enough. A real man and father will give his child's needs top priority. Also, without your guidance, your child has a high chance of running the streets. Eventually, your child will make a lot of mistakes or even become a teen dad. Kids having kids continues the vicious cycle. If you do not want your child to be a teen daddy, hold up your values and do not become a teen daddy yourself.

Not listening to your parents and not staying in school are as bad as heading down the wrong lane. You know the result? Head-on collisions with a high possibility of injuries and fatalities.

Using profanity to get attention is seeking attention in the wrong way. Vulgar language discounts who you ought to be.

Always being late to scheduled appointments is bad. Respect others' time and do not keep them waiting. Earn others' respect and maintain a reputation as a person who is punctual.

Not being gentlemanly and chivalrous are signs of being crude and not polished. Show discipline by accepting and practicing social etiquette. If you are polished, you will gain many more admirers.

The short-term gratification of being a bully is not worth the long-term pain and disappointment. Many bullies are not as successful in life as those they bullied.

Do a self-check by looking into the mirror. If you are not one of the favorites of the weaker boys or the not-so-beautiful girls in your class, you are either mean or oppressive to them. Whatever it is, change it for the better. You can do better. Respect everyone. Respect begets respect. You will be much happier being known as a gentle soul than as a bully.

The character you cultivate in your younger years will follow you.

It pays to be good to others. Do not burn bridges because you may need one of the bridges to cross life's rushing river.

You may never see most of your high school classmates again, but some of them will cross paths with you as if you had a planned rendezvous. While you may not see most of them again, the ones you do encounter could be the ones you dread meeting.

You will find out high school friends take a special place in your memory stacks. Friends from that time until your early thirties tend to be more enduring than others. Of course, only a few people are as good as old friends. And, yes, no one replaces nobody.

Be friends with many people, and as much as possible, avoid making enemies. You will be surprised that those people in your early life may be the lending hands propelling you into the orbit holding your destiny. The values and habits you built by high school graduation will lay the foundation to your character.

Avoid unforced errors. Like a wheel hub, one turn will deserve another. And like a boat, if you take on water, you will eventually sink. How you carry yourself will determine whether you enjoy inward peace of mind or not. And your outward display will be out there for the world to see.

Your character is your honor. And if your honor is not worth safeguarding, what is? You compromise your honor and integrity—and you will quickly discover that evil seeks companions. You do not want to be in the unenvious situation where you will be asked if you are guilty or not guilty.

It pays to be a person with a good reputation. Manage your persona and your real character. Look inside out and outside in to understand your situation. Decide what you stand for and what you stand against. Be comfortable in your own skin. A key ingredient to honorable character is being truthful to yourself and others.

Do not exhaust yourself by comparing yourself to others because you really do not know their life journey. Yes, do not dwell on others' character—dwell on yours and watch your own lane.

If you are humble, you will not stumble. Even if you stumble, be among the first to admit it. If appropriate, laugh about it. Do not take life too seriously. None of us is checking out of this world alive. The world is a playground—and you will go home at some point.

Always introduce yourself to the crowd—and never assume everyone knows you. When you are wrong, accept that you are wrong—and accept that it is your fault. Accept your problems as your own because no one else will. Take responsibility for your actions. Part of being humble is knowing when to say sorry. Being graceful and appreciative goes a long way. Not taking yourself too seriously and laughing along with others at your expense is laudable. Absence of a condescending attitude toward others makes it easy for them to come to you.

Listen attentively when you listen; the front, back, and stories in between all matter. And when you speak, choose your words carefully and speak with piety and respect.

As a humble person, you should know beauty is only skin deep. And everyone's feelings can be hurt. You should keep things in perspective. Everyone's viewpoint is relative to the situation. Treat others as you want to be treated.

Some things are assumed to be very simple and common knowledge, yet many people get them wrong. A specific case in point is tipping those in consumer service. Waiters in restaurants and others who rely heavily on the kindness of your heart and the tips you leave them generally feel tips less than 10 percent of your bill are not OK. Do better, give more if you can, and put a smile in your service provider's heart. Completely forgoing a tip is ungentlemanly. Do not tolerate anyone who skips it. Do not be the one who doesn't tip.

Your everyday good gestures to others may not show up on the statistics sheet, but they speak volumes about who you are, your reputation, and how good you feel.

Talk *to* people and not *at* people. Communication skills are extremely important in relating well to others. Your word is your worth, and your worth is your word. When you breach your words, you become a fraud—and fraudsters lack honor.

Be a Good Samaritan. Always ask others, particularly the helpless, how you can help them.

Surf the high ocean waves of helping others and enjoy the soothing feeling of knowing you have made another person's day better. It is better to hear someone laughing than crying. It feels good when you know you are a factor in the happy moment.

You are special and have your own lock combination. Unlock the good in you, roar on your eight cylinders, and to pull others up and along.

Fulfill your purpose in life. It will be a deliberate effort. Your success in life will not be an accident; it will be because you made it so.

A stitch in time saves nine—and the earlier you start holding yourself accountable the better. Water only drowns someone in the water. If you cannot swim, avoid diving into deep water. Why jump into a boat going nowhere? You cannot save yourself when you are buried.

Be wary of advice from shady characters. A drowning person do not try to save another drowning person. Blaming others for your demise is like medicine after death; it is useless.

Now is the time to listen to your inner voice. Take constructive criticism from those with poise who truly mean you well. You are the captain of your own boat. You are responsible for piloting yourself to the winner's cycle or the pile of underperformers.

You can take a horse to the stream, but you cannot force the horse to drink. If you get mad and drown the horse, you have a much bigger problem. Besides walking home, you are a textbook example of animal cruelty.

The mice that take the bait of a hissing snake become meals. The principles you hold will help you stay rational and keep your emotions in check. Avoid the things you do with very high emotions. You may regret them when your emotions flatline.

Sometimes, hold your tongue and enjoy the madness. Not saying what you want to say until the right time is a sign of maturity. Also, put your "that is the way we used to do it syndrome" in check. What was done in the past and how it was done may not be relevant today because the new order has overtaken it. Do not resort to finding fault; it is one of the easiest things to do.

In your utterances, be sensitive and respectful to others' feelings. Mutual respect and understanding go a long way toward being relatable. Do not be a shiny object with nothing underneath the hood.

If you lack values, your character will lack constitution. You will go in whatever direction the wind blows. Without grounding values, you will not run like a well-oiled machine. Learn proper values and have a strong moral compass.

Do you know yourself? Take inventory of your values. There is a problem when you waffle or vacillate on issues. Have a position. Do your best not to compromise your core values—they are the fabric of your character—and never sell your values for popularity.

Manage Life's Troubles

Your character is the sum of your values, how you manage your life troubles, and the people you hang around.

Any time and energy spent making a trouble-free life is not lost. Your parents' genes will be passed on to you. That definitely will impact your character. You will take after your mother and father in one form or another. Fruit does not fall far from the parent tree. The parents' lifestyle and environment during their kids' formative years will contribute to defining their kids' character. Monkey see, monkey do.

What can you do if you don't like what you see? Being aware and recognizing the situation is a great start. Change whatever characteristics of your parents that you find flawed or offensive. Do not repeat that conduct—and avoid it like a plague. Avoid the bad things that other older adults do around you. Never repeat the mistakes they made. Learn from them. If you fail at first, get up, dust yourself off, regroup, and try to do better.

With the best of what your parents gave you, improve your stake. Leverage nurture—self-made, as much as possible—to compensate for your nature and genetic predispositions. Exploit your environment as much as feasible. Manage your situation with the goal of being in a better position than where you started. You can do better. Never accept being mediocre.

Occasionally, you might find yourself in the crosshairs of trouble. What will you do? Fight or take flight? Ask yourself if a hill is worth dying for? Only a few things are worth dying for. Those things are bigger than your own interests. Greater good for the masses is a noble cause. Do not get lost in the irony of a situation.

Live for something. Pick your battles. Everything and every day should not be a crisis. Prioritize. It is important to find a way to live to fight another day. Tomorrow will be a new day. The choices you make will make up your character.

What you like and do not like are on display in your choices. If your choices are messed up, your internal filters and values are probably messed up too. When you make truth your cardinal guide, most of your choices will be right on target. Also, making choices will be easier. You can choose yes for the truth or no for lies. Simple. No matter the outcome, you should follow the truth.

If you are wobbly or tend to be neutral, you will have a bigger problem facing you. It is difficult to remain neutral because you can be knocked down by traffic from either side. You are more likely to second-guess yourself, and subject yourself to the should-have, would-have, and could-have state of mind. In neutral, your vehicle can roll, which is an accident waiting to happen. You do not want that restlessness. Strive to be in an affirmative or negative position—not neutral. In the real world, you cannot stay neutral for long before man-made forces bend you and push you off to a side.

The choice is yours. Your actions and choices cast your action mold. Over time, your action patterns will entrench in your being and become your habits. These habits become your character. Because you are what you repeatedly do, your character becomes your destiny.

It is your choice to be enthusiastic about life. It is your choice to have a passion for something. Capitalize on your enthusiasm and passion to build a solid character and see your destiny come through.

Do not meander around what needs to be done. Good or bad, it is your choice. For consolation, nature does not often make straight lines.

Your choices will stare at you from every corner. The cost for bad choices is a troubled pathway, which never goes away by itself.

To finish right, make the right choices and build the right character from the onset.

Commit to doing the right things. There is no right way to do the wrong things. It will cost you more not to do what is right—and besides the wrong done, you have sold your soul too.

Disregard the many reasons why you cannot do the right things. Instead, find one reason why you should do the right thing—and do it. After choosing to do the right things, you must follow up by doing those right things the right way. Doing the right things the wrong way can create problems like robbing Peter to pay Paul. No matter the excuses, wrong is wrong. And no matter who does it, wrong is still wrong.

If you tolerate wrongs, they will metastasize. Without uprooting the weeds from the roots, the weeds regrow.

Rearranging the chairs to keep a sinking ship from going down may give you a false sense of safety. In a matter of time, your unsound decisions will catch up with you and send you and the ship into the abyss.

The enemy has a vote too. The enemy can detect your weakest point and latch onto your jugular as opportunity allows. Solid character will help your focus be where it needs to be, and it will save you from floundering and blunders.

Plan ahead to improve your odds in favor of trouble-free days. You do not have enough daylight in your lifetime to do everything you want to do. Do not waste any of that time on trouble. Plan your days, weeks, months, and years. Have your plans nested like one building block to another.

There is no need to schedule every hour of the day. Leave some white space for reflection and retraining. Your choice may be to do less better or do more is more. Don't do anything haphazardly. Make your primary focus one key thing a day, a set of things per week, a set of things per month, and one major thing a year.

No plan survives the first contact, but having no plan is worse. Without plans, you are more likely to lose your mooring and wander aimlessly through the wilderness of life.

Your plans may not go as planned, but you can adjust them as the days unfold. Work hard and play hard—but keep the focus where it needs to be. Waste no energy or time trying to grab smoke. Never choose to die on a hill that is already abandoned. You do not have the luxury of eternity. You have an allotted time on planet earth. What you do with it is your choice. Do not take the days you have on earth for granted. Wasting time is akin to wasting your life. Are you killing time because of laziness? Procrastination allows your problems to grow.

Killing your own time is akin to suicide—not murder. In any case, say no to murder—and say *hell no* to suicide. You need to do right with your time and everything else.

Apportion your time in the most effective way to make things happen. An option could be spending 10 percent on lessons from yesterday's events, 60 percent on getting today's best results, and the remaining 30 percent on preparing for tomorrow's growth.

No matter how you slice it, you only have twenty-four hours a day, seven days a week, maybe thirty days a month, and 365 days in a year. Only a handful of people get to live to be a centenarian and witness that much time passing. Your time on earth is numbered. You cannot turn your life clock back. Once it has passed, it is in the past. Like water under the bridge, you cannot bring it back—and you cannot bring back time that had ticked past.

Be careful. Haste makes waste. Measure twice and cut once. Avoid cutting corners. If you do things right the first time around, you will save time. While the right choices will help you keep trouble at bay, luck is part of the formula—and that cannot be overlooked. Improve your luck by envisioning the majority of your problems before you have them on your doorstep. Doing so will help you tackle yesterday's problem yesterday, today's problem today, and tomorrow's problem tomorrow.

Plan your work—and then work your plan. If you happen to make mistakes, learn quickly and adjust your fire. It is great if the fair winds find you, but do not blame others for the mistakes you made while running into the headwinds.

Give your best effort to your everyday decisions, and you will have no regrets about what you accomplished compared to what you think you should have accomplished. Your goal should be excellence and not perfection. Perfection is rare; even the salesmen of the year fail to always get others to bite the dust on their bidding.

Don't trouble trouble until trouble troubles you.

Let a sleeping lion lie. Respect the king of the jungle and his domain. Respect his attitude. You will pay for trying to touch his tail. If you grab a cat by the tail, you are likely to be mauled. You invite ants into your home when you bring home infested wood. Make it your character not to trouble trouble until trouble troubles you.

Making everything trouble is trouble. Worrying gives a small thing a big shadow. It makes you to run away from something that is not after you. It may put things in your mind and make you see things that are not there. Sound familiar?

Worrying never fixes anything. Your worries are self-perceived problems, and they can knock you out or make you miss your own party.

Check the fear that causes you to make excuses, particularly when you have to swim against the current. Avoid false starts and nervous energy. Do not whimper and quit before you jump into the water. Your fears can be irrational, or they can be progressive.

You may take counsel from your fears, but never allow it to douse your action or quench your flame with carbon dioxide. Be courageous. Physical and moral courage result in virtue.

When you lie, you have to remember your lies or lie even more to cover your original lies. You will eventually be entangled in the web of your own lies. That is trouble.

You will find yourself in bondage because you will always be on the lookout. Are your defensive lies leaking oil? Being on guard all the time will leave you winded and drained.

Are you known for not keeping your word? Lying causes people to look at you like you have egg yolk smeared on your forehead. That is self-made trouble.

Being consistently inconsistent is not a badge of honor you want to wear. Rust consumes iron, and lying will subject you to stress and cracks, and it will eventually break you. Big lies and little lies leave black marks on your reputation. Forsake lies in all your ways to be free from the shackles of lies. If you are truthful with yourself, you can say the truth anytime. You never have to try to remember your earlier lies.

If you are known for always telling the truth, you are more likely to enjoy the trust of your superiors and peers. Excellence is contagious, and your examples will motivate your subordinates. You will feel much better knowing you are trusted by the people who know you.

Honesty is still the best policy. Truth is constant, but with lies, you have to invent more lies or remember old lies, which is much harder. If you need ground to stand on, that ground is truth.

Your life journey is akin to a long-distance run. It is not a sprint. There is no easy way out of the marathon. You must pound your share of the pavement to strengthen your legs and build endurance.

Address your trouble spots before the marathon. The price for not being prepared is disqualification or quitting. Be sure to train and invest for the long haul.

You are responsible for your character and success. Make progress—not excuses. Do not be the type who finds many ways to be distracted.

Do not spread yourself too thin. It is better to be above average at something than to be a jack-of-all-trades and master of none. Nobody is an expert in everything they do. Find your niche and be good at it. Divide the labor; be good at some things, and let others be good at the rest. Trying to do everything, pleasing everyone, and claiming to know everything is a recipe for failure. Learn to leave weaving to the beaver, the orchestra to the conductor, and movies to the actors. Know when to say no, not now, and never. Know when others are best situated for the task at hand—and hand it off to them appropriately. Life offers a lot of trip wires. Expect the unexpected troubles. No one goes through life without scratches. No one is infallible. Go to the game to play and win. The definite way to lose is to quit before the game starts.

If you use your brain and heart to choose the right things and do the right things, you are likely to be OK. You will not spend too much time checking the rearview mirror.

Taking no actions and making no changes does not mean things around you will not change. Life's troubles are always alive and well. Do not be blasé about shenanigans. Living life requires you to be alert, adaptive, and relevant before you become obsolete and get deleted.

You have to adjust your sails when you cannot change the direction of the winds. Otherwise, you may never get to your destination. When you stop changing, you stop growing. Change brings growth.

Only fools never change their minds. Do not let your opinions hold you hostage. Build your character and be one who avoids extremes. Stay in balance. Continue learning, growing, and changing. Master the art of bouncing back. Stumbling blocks and stepping stones are there for a reason. Apprenticeship.

Your takeaway from each experience in life to a large extent depends upon your reactions. They can be positive or negative. It is best to use your reactions to reshape the situations in your favor.

Foolish decisions will shackle your life. Never beat or rape a woman. If you do, jail time is in your future. The traumatized remain traumatized forever, and the record follows you for the rest of your life. Your good intentions don't matter; what matters is if you violated another person or the law. Unless you want to be dragged to hell and back, avoid momentary gratification from foolhardy actions.

Beware of binging on alcohol. When you are drunk, everything looks good. You will ignore logic and foul up. The golden eagle looks majestic until you see one with plugged feathers. You may not be able to tell it from a featherless vulture. Trouble will cost you those feathers. If you want to keep the majestic look, you have to keep the feathers by keeping trouble at bay.

We are born equal, but we are different. Some arrive in this world with their bread well buttered. You will know these people when you see them. These individuals only need to do a little to live in luxury. Others come into this world with troubles that make one question God's intent.

Some people are born to parents with very modest means, and the basic living essentials are outside their means. Others are born in environments and locations that are devoid of the comfort creatures of life. Even worse are those with debilitating medical conditions. These situations force them to become comfortable being uncomfortable.

Yes, nature has spoken. Hold no bitterness.

You are where you are for a reason. It is by design and not by cosmic accident. You will see things as you are. The troubles you avoid or go through will give you a different perspective. Just be who you see yourself as and try to stand out. You are who you were born to be. Try to reach your potential. Just as a tea bag is only useful in hot water and a locomotive is powerful on the rail but weak off it, you must deliberately apply yourself to reach your potential. There are opportunities everywhere. They are waiting for an observant eye to discover them. Look for them.

So many successful people were not born with gold spoons in their mouths. They got very good at what they are brilliant at. They know what is important today and tomorrow. With hard work and some luck, they mastered the strokes of success and fixed their trouble spots. One for the books, a worthy case study, is Tyler Perry, a self-made billionaire. The American actor, producer, and entertainment mogul's story shows that where there is a will, there is a way.

Being successful has its perks. Once you fly first class, economy seats will look like half-baked bread. Go out there and be you—onstage extrovert, offstage introvert, or otherwise. The sun's rays do not burn until they are brought into focus. Take action and fan the flames of your success. When you procrastinate, you dig a grave for your good intentions. Believe you can—and then do it.

Now is all you have, do not let trouble distract you. There is no time like the present, and there is no present like time. Are you doing all you can do with your now? Find ways to make your now count toward the future, and it will come one day at a time.

Success may appear to come overnight, but it does not. It is the sum of the little steps you have taken. Rome was not built in one day. Be prepared and invest to win. Be ready to seize opportunities that are out of reach of many people. Go beyond swimming downstream. Swim upstream to the prize. Most of the time, you win by chasing down a moving target.

Expect rivalries—they will keep you on your toes.

Trust your instinct. Good or bad, own it.

Recognize opportunities and solve problems. Obstacles can be detours, but only you can stop you. Obstacles are part of life—do not let them hold you prisoner. Do your best. Is your best the best that can be done? If not, do more. There is still room for improvement.

Talk yourself up. Think about the impact and results of your contributions. Never let success go to your head. If you do, people will look at you like someone who forgot to brush their teeth.

You may not be able to bring the water under the bridge back, but do not let past mistakes become memorials that make you feel hollow. Do not forget that yesterday died last night. It is more important to ensure you are headed in the right direction while making the mistake.

Persevere. Rise up when you are knocked down. Do not fall before you are pushed. Trying times are not the time to get tied. You may fight a battle more than once to win it. Opportunities often hide behind obstacles. The last key in the bunch can be the one that opens the lock.

There is a "but" in everything. Deciding when to invoke it is your call. Your choice may be to forget it, go around it, go over it, go under it, or go through it to accomplish life's purpose. You may give in and let the "but" stop your progress. Your choice.

Your self-image, self-esteem, and superiority or inferiority complex will determine your comfort zone.

How you feel depends on who you are comparing yourself to. It is best to compare yourself to the standards and not people.

With the good choices you make, you will be in a position to manage your troubles. What you lack in quantity, you can make up in quality. You should value the things you acquire more than the things that are given to you. Every person has a story to tell, but a tree falling in the forest may not be heard by anyone.

Your words and deeds are your story, and they connect you to others. Being on a team helps showcase your story. Belong in the right social circle. If you have a choice, a community of brave men and women is the team to belong to. These folks remain calm in the face of fear and danger. They live for what they believe in, and they know life is more than pleasure. Just as they will run toward gunfire without hesitation to rescue a team member, they will validate your story and shout it from the rooftops. Associate yourself with people who can multiply you and your story.

Your mass-produced education combined with your hand-crafted live lessons will allow you to create your own life systems. You can weave in the tapestry of your voice to say what others do not say about you. So, contribute to the world by making a difference with your story.

What excites you? If you do not stand up for something, you will fall for anything. Your beliefs and convictions are your filters. You live the life you choose, and you define your own success.

Talk is cheap. You make excuses to cage yourself in and live it. Many things catch your eyes, but a few catch your heart. If you have a passion for something, you will be ready to give it your all and more. Your attitude alters your abilities.

Keep up your enthusiasm and passion for life. If you don't, you will stagnate and become hopeless. Being happy and enthusiastic is a choice. Find your own unique voice for your choices, decisions, actions, and inactions. Seize initiatives and be committed. Be more on the offense than on the defense.

Do not be afraid to fail. When you fail, try a new approach. We all have blind spots and fail sometimes, and no one likes to be compared to a failure. Be the one who learns from your mistakes. Failure and success are products of the same process. Practice draws from experience to reduce the failure rate. Try to master the moment.

You will have trouble when you treat others with contempt. You are not an emperor. You are not a god. Treat others as you want to be treated.

Everybody faces troubles. Everyone has a tipping point, a trigger point, and a pain point. Everybody experiences friction in life. You have to be empathetic to understand these situations.

Keep troubles in perspective and in context.

Just as engineers understand construction mechanics and don't blame water for flowing down, it is never good to blame people for their pain. Show people you care. Do not be uppity in your relations. Make time for people to talk to you. Give them deserving attention. Listen rather than thinking about what to say. Emphasizing your similarity with them will build a unifying bond.

Let your character speak loudly and clearly and show others that you are a vessel to move their agenda. If they believe you truly care, they will help you when you begin the hard work of fixing trouble.

Tempers lead to trouble. Don't be hot under the collar. Never let your temper be like dynamite setting fire and consuming a forest. No matter how hot-tempered you are, your temper cannot boil water or cook beans. A hot temper will bring out the worst of you.

When you leave people hanging in the cold, their love for you will turn malignant and metastasize into hate.

Embrace being polite. Recognize others' presence and give them their due respect. Embrace the power of saying thank you and you're welcome. Know when to say excuse me, pardon me, and please. Never forget politeness is an antidote for relational incompetence.

Be contrite if you make a mistake. Accept your mistake. Say why you can do better. Say what you will do better.

Your tongue is a weapon, and it can cause trouble. Be careful with what you do with your tongue and your gestures. What comes out of your mouth can be more hurtful than physically inflicted pain. Time may heal physical wounds, but the scars from virulent words remain much longer.

When others perform, it is your choice to praise or criticize them. Choose the former. If you are going to complain about something, offer solutions to improve the situation. If you must, only criticize humbly—and do not try to correct everything. It is better to be known as someone who solves problems than someone who creates problems. Be the answer. Find solutions. If need be, hold out an olive branch.

Pour oil on troubled water. Love looks through a telescope, and envy looks through a microscope. People tend to love the people who love them.

Never leave a trail of hurt people. Allow other people to win arguments. If you treat people well, they are more likely to treat you well in return.

Approve of others. Forgive and forget. You would not bite a dog because the dog bit you. When you forgive, you will be happy that you are no longer carrying the burden. If you choose revenge, what do you do after the revenge? Your anger may subside, but your happiness may never return.

Be welcoming. Be a good person. Look for a way to give and serve those who do not have the power to return the favor. Help others succeed with their passions. Help people get where they are going. Make someone feel important. Help someone make a difference. Helping others succeed is noble.

Give more than you take. Your happiness will be equal to how much service you give others. What you have dies with you, but what you give to others lives on. Hunt for the good in people and help them get better. We all, at times, need help from somebody.

The world needs kindness. Pass it on—even with small deeds. Share from the heart.

People may not know you personally, but they will never forget what you did for them. They will never forget your kindness. Does Abraham Lincoln's name ring a bell? What you did to help others or your community will be remembered forever.

In life, people will move in and out of your orbit. Expect to deal with the drama of imperfect people. Things mean different things to different people in different places and different times. When you are absent-minded, dealing with others can be critical to the results you see.

See others as you want to be seen. Do not judge others by their disabilities, ethnicities, what they wear, live, or drive, or how they speak. Do not be the person who always sees others as obstacles. People and time are among your best assets.

Do not be alone on the mountaintop. Bring your teammates along; you will need them to survive troubled times.

Reflect. What are you doing right or wrong? Ask people around you the tough question: "How am I doing?"

Beg them not to let you fall on your face. Let your demeanor signal your openness to welcome and accept constructive criticism. Hear them out. Break and replace any noted vices.

When people who know how you walk, how you speak, and how you behave, think you are doing something stupid, listen and stop immediately. You may be in trouble.

It is important to know your strengths, but it is more important to know your weaknesses.

There are a lot of things you cannot see about yourself, but those who know you well can recognize your profile from a mile away.

If you pay deaf ears to their concerns, you may end up in a circular firing squad. When the noise settles, if you are alive, you will wish you had listened.

Take advantage of the camera of history. It is much easier for old eyes to find old routes, but a new set of eyes can see overlooked things and find new meaning in old things. It is going to take a different kind of thinking to get you out of it than to get you into it. Your reputation in life will not take form by magic. It takes energy and time to build a reputation. Your vocation and lifestyle will be in play. You will demonstrate that you can compete, cooperate, and graduate.

Your emotional math is in play in your relationships. Remain attentive because one lousy moment can send your reputation crashing down. People are watching. Given the challenges of finding your true self—your best self—imagine the chance of succeeding in changing others. Many others are going through life's growing pains. Therefore, make an honest effort to be more tolerant of other people's situations before passing judgments.

It is never good to quickly see others in a negative light or assume they have maligned motives. Get along and go along as needed. Act with excitement and enthusiasm and leave a favorable impression on people. Smile because your smile makes others smile. Smile because you are happy to be alive. Your smile adds to your face value, and you need no prescription for that.

Bring along people of all stripes to smile with you in your moment in the sun. Your warmness or lack of it will determine how much you can win over people's emotions and sway their logic in your favor.

Your ears are not there for beauty. They are there to hear. Listen to what others are saying. Make it a priority to listen to everyone who talks to you. Listen for things you know and things you do not know. You do not learn when you are talking.

Poor relationships will be a jugular attack to your character and public standing. The quicker you learn how to manage your relationships, the better.

Choose goals that support your character. Be willing to exchange a piece of your life for them. Do what you can do before what you cannot do. Focus on what you can control—and never let your weaknesses get in the way of your strengths.

Never feel ashamed about trying and failing. Whoever never failed never tried. Failures quit when they fail, and winners continue to fail until they succeed. A trouble that does not kill you will make you stronger. Do your best to handle small troubles before they become bigger troubles. Small troubles are part of the rungs to help you go up or down life's ladder.

No one like people who start off with why they cannot do stuff. Do not allow a bottleneck to bar you from finding a way to get things done. The road to success runs uphill. The path of least resistance makes a river crooked. Interstate highways are only possible because engineers defied the oddities of the natural terrain and managed them to their advantage. A path with no obstacles leads nowhere. Look at where you are and what you can become.

Your future depends on many things, mostly on how you manage your troubles. One of your goals should be to be happy doing good things. True happiness is an inside job; your impactful efforts reward you with peace of mind.

Another goal should be to fill your brain with something useful. Commit your brain—your powerhouse—to work. Learn something new every day. Your brain will thank you. Who wants to be living with the eerie echo of an empty room? There will be some roadblocks and detours as you are driving on the highways of your life journey. You cannot run over the roadblocks and expect to get to your destination in peace. If you want to get to your destination in pieces, go ahead and disobey the road rules. Bad idea, bad choice.

Many products come with assembly, maintenance, and troubleshooting instructions, but you came with none. Instead of spinning the dial of life blindly and hoping for a lucky break, study and emulate those who have already done it. Call up the fact witnesses. Determine if they have new information and provide the missing link. The witnesses are not always nuns and school librarians—be judicious and not judicial in what you take in and leave out. The wisdom you gather from those tested and proven witnesses will offer you success.

Your hard work in learning and applying what you have learned will help you manage your troubles and achieve your desired results much faster. People all around the world with humble beginnings have made it big. Look where you are, and you will find a few. Never let a deprived background shackle your dream of being a success. Build your own dream; otherwise, someone will hire you to build theirs. Do you get it?

People born with silver spoons in their mouths do not have a monopoly on success. Study success in its many forms, choose your life path, and cast your die. Remain morally and ethically grounded. Follow your passion. Discipline and consistency will be necessary to get you to the finish line.

Track your habits and line them up with the character you want to represent you. Keep to your daily goals, weekly goals, monthly goals, and yearly goals. Do not accept movement as progress. Always ask yourself if your measurement of effectiveness is on par. If not, adjust, reengage, and do better.

How you think about a situation determines how you feel, and how you feel will determine your behavior. If you yearn to be the greatest of all time, your inner being will propel your outer experience and your actions. Your actions and reactions are rarely accidents. Watch your thinking. It signals what consumes you and the road you want to take. Are you thinking right? If you manage your thinking, you will manage your feelings. You will act like you feel. If you act nobly, you are likely to feel good and happy. Bingo. Decide what is right for you. Decide what makes your heart happy before you decide what is possible.

Some of your life experiences will change you forever. Make peace with the past so you do not spoil the present. While it may make sense to visit the past, do not stay there.

Excuses will not absolve you from being culpable for your crimes. If you live by hook or by crook, you will eventually be in hot water. Taking the laws into your own hands may expose you to retribution, which you may regret.

Beware of achieving an objective by any means possible. Doing it could bankrupt your ethical and moral purse.

Your earlier actions in life will cast your die as a reputable or non-reputable character. And once you cross the Rubicon, your day of reckoning will stare at you like an invisible monster. Do not make your situation worse by jumping from the frying pan to the fire. An autopsy tells the dead person's story. People do not take their own lives and hide themselves.

Because criminals often operate in their zone of familiarity, for the investigative eyes, mundane clues properly put together often break open a case. No wonder criminals are never too smart to evade the law forever.

Mind your own business. If you live in a glass house, you should not throw stones. You may be paid in kind. Avoid giving a dog a bad name and hanging him. Karma may pay you a visit. If you want an eye for an eye, you may be paid in kind.

When you smell a rat, particularly at the eleventh hour, follow your sixth sense and play it safe. All that glistens is not gold. You have to read between the lines. Prevention is better than a cure; when possible, avoid living on the fault line.

No one is immune to problems. Even soaring bald eagles occasionally face mobs of crows. Lions in the African grassland fight flies and less intimidating carnivores. Gazelles have to run faster than the fastest leopard to survive.

Humans have our own unique problems. Our ecosystem demands we remain vigilant to avoid becoming the prey. Problems are part and parcel of life. It was here before you, and it will be here after you.

You get up, and you walk by faith. Have faith that you are capable. Have faith in your ability to see beyond things that do not exist physically. Along your walk, you will go through transformative stages like a butterfly in gestation. Baby. Child. Adult. Senior. That is your life course, and there are unique challenges in each stage. Manage your expectations.

When people gather together, someone is usually the center of attention. It is the bride in a wedding ceremony, the deceased at a funeral, or a defendant in the court system. Know who the story is about—and respect the order of things. Are you that awkward character who gives a standing ovation at a funeral?

Are you sneezing on someone's birthday cake? Are you dancing and screaming the most to get attention? Are you the skydiver parachuting in to be the story on other people's days?

Do not be the drunk and act like hurricane, which does not spare geographical boundaries. If you do, your mistakes will have consequences. A hand grenade blows itself up before blowing up everybody within its kill zone. Do not be a hand grenade to be the center of attention at the expense of someone else.

Mind your etiquette and conduct. Respect other people's spaces. Your freedom is not absolute when it hurts others. While cherishing your freedom, never abuse your liberty.

Pulling the rug from underneath a friend's feet is not the best way to make a joke. What about putting your friend in a position to catch a double-edged knife? Did you consider your friend's freedom to be part of your act? No matter your reasons, the result is the same. If you are self-absorbed, you are likely to lose your friends. Your reputation will precede you wherever you go.

When it rains, it gets muddy. In a marsh, the earthworms come out—and the crabs come out to eat them. Life is a game of natural selection, but do not make matters worse than they already are by wiping out those habitats.

Robbing Peter to pay Paul is false justice. How would you feel to be visited with false justice? What goes around comes around. Sooner or later, you will discover robbery is akin to an ill wind that blows no one good.

If you stir up the hornet's nest, be ready for the sting. If you swallow a poison pill, it is just a matter of time before it will get you. Once the cat is out of the bag, you have lost control. Never hit a man when he is down or flog a dead horse. False justice goes against normal human decency.

Don't sabotage your life. Watch out for emptiness. An empty bag will hardly stand upright. When your brain is empty, the devil will find a way to rent it as a workshop and turn your character devious. The importance of denying the devil a home in you is priceless. Occupying your brain with solid precepts—rules guiding your thoughts and behaviors—is priceless.

Be honorable, call a spade a spade, having one foot in a restricted area is one too many, and strike while the iron is hot. Be more than good—be great. The first to the hill chooses where to sit. You cannot shoe a running horse. You decline when you rest on your laurels. If you complain, you explain. If you never complain, you never explain. If you explain, you are losing. Half a loaf is better than no bread. It is not what happened that matters the most; it is how you see what happened. Do not burn down the house to renovate the kitchen. When you do bad things in secret, remember that walls have ears. The autopsy tells the story the killer leaves out. Investigators know when the math doesn't add up, and they look for the smoke because where there is smoke, there is fire. If your lifestyle reflects these precepts, you will be a model character.

It is bad when others describe you with these words: misogynist (women hater), racist (race-based hater), xenophobic (foreigner hater), anti-Semitic (Jewish hater), Islamophobic (anti-Muslim), homophobic (gay hater), or chauvinist (superiority complex). This list is not all-inclusive. Search your soul for the red flags and repent.

Once you repent and discard those acquired beliefs, you will cease running from your own shadow. Do not be that character. Don't be a sardine can that is packed with versions of hate. Do not live the limited number of years you have on earth hating other people. Love thy neighbor.

Are you sabotaging yourself? If you commit crimes, you will ruin your victim's life and your own life. If you fatally hurt another person, you will quickly discover that tragedy compounds tragedy. You will alter the destiny of your loved ones and many more. Your evil deed will put others in situations that are like being inside a tornado. Your crimes will put a heavy lid on the doors of people's life journeys. Your crime will put you on a fast-forward flirtation with your demise.

Your dog-eat-dog excuse will break apart when it is subjected to the intense heat of peering eyes. The skeleton in your closet will eventually be found. Your lies will be more incriminating than exonerating. Your cop-out—blaming others—will fall flat on its face. Once caught, you will feel like a fish out of water. You will bite the dust soon afterward. Crime is the kiss of death; it will suffocate you and never leave you.

Are you sabotaging others? Group norms are not holy sanctimony. The acquiescence of a male-dominated workforce and unequal pay for women speaks to this fact. Competence is competence, and it deserves equal recognition. We can never have enough competent people; there is space upstairs. There is enough for everybody's needs if it were not for people's greed. Just be fair.

You may stand by and witness gentrification. Low-income inhabitants are displaced by richer tenants—without even raising eyebrows. If you see something, you should say something. Those in authority must seek the neighborhood activists' mitigation plans to reach a compromise and accommodate them as quickly as possible. Not everybody is going to be happy.

There is no sugarcoating it; a lie is a lie. Inaction is acquiescence. Every situation is different, and success is different for everyone. Oppression of any sort is horrible. Pray that you are never on the receiving end. Do everything you can to change things that are wrong and never oppress others.

What you do is more important than what you say. The ripple effects of your contributions will make the world a better place.

Be aware of implicit bias. A community conscience can make a group not admit they have blind spots. A group may wrap itself in the bondage of hypocrisy and find reasons to justify their repressive ways. These are all man-made impediments because people forget or neglect humanity. Everyone bleeds and feels pain.

If something looks amiss, it is probably amiss. There will definitely be times when things are not together. Why are those folks being treated unfairly or poorly? When your heart throbs and your inner voice tells you something is wrong, something is really wrong. Raise your concerns to the powers that be in private before going public. Wrongdoing is not OK yesterday, today, or tomorrow.

Be a pioneer—stand out as an advocate for what is right. You may be attacked, but do not buckle under pressure. Protest against illegal, unethical, and immoral acts. History will be on your side when the stories of those who gave their all for the common good are told. You will emerge as the giant of your time like Abraham Lincoln, Martin Luther King, and Nelson Mandela. Being mentioned in the same sentence as those historic characters is an achievement in itself.

Do not be afraid to be different when you are in the right. Lean on your moral courage and deny fear the oxygen it needs to consume you. Have the courage to step into the unknown and speak up. Practice calling people in before calling them out. Help rewrite the playbook, positively touch people you meet along the way, and make yourself unforgettable. Try to make people feel better.

In an ideal world, we would all be ideal, but an ideal world is a fallacy. You do not live in a bubble where you are the alpha and omega. Others live in the world too, and they vote. Your zip code can determine where you end up. It is naïve to deny that societal inequities exist. You are not immune to the contagion, but you can choose to be a dropout or a contributing member of the society. Choose to be an impactful gentleman.

Avoid sabotaging others. Instead, enable others. The long line of people who sold out their consciences will collect dust in the ashes of history and take their place in the infamous roster, your good deeds shall forever be remembered adorably when history unfolds.

Like it or not, life is a centrifugal force, and it is exerting itself on you. The days and nights come and go as weeks, months, and years. They are wrapped up in the seasons of the year: winter, spring, summer, and fall. Some of these periods are rainy, and some are dry. The environment responds to these seasonal changes. Grasses grow or die, foliage falls, and trees bloom. Migratory birds follow the clock too. Humans are more depressed during the winter, and they are happier when winter is over. Why is this important? Program your character to match.

Your memorable teachers and classmates are more likely to enter your life between kindergarten and young adulthood. A few exceptions may occur at forty or beyond. Looking back, these encounters will bring memories of good and bad times. You may want to repress some of those memories forever, and you might want to relive others. You will remember your neighbors from childhood until their memories fade away.

The public figures and activities (politics, sports, entertainment, business, and religion) you grew up with can date you. The fashion of the day and age-appropriate styles provide road markers on your journey. Bell-bottom jeans, tight jeans, flat shoes, and classic or modern-cut clothes represent different segments of your journey.

Each decade has a dominant music genre: rock, pop, hip-hop, country, rhythm and blues, and soul. Most likely, you will be in tune with the popular music of your time. Your musical taste, genres, and artists will give up your generation.

Even the style and furnishings in your home tell stories. Your communities will evolve too. Your cities, counties, states, and countries will evolve as well. If you pay attention, you will witness the changes as they happen. The oceans, continents, and environments are changing too. Some of the changes appear to be on a linear scale, and others appear to be on an exponential scale. If you have an inquisitive mind, you want to know what is going on around you.

You are an unfinished product in an unfinished world. Things look different than they did a decade ago. Do not even think about comparing today to a century ago. Each new day brings its own opportunities and challenges. To make situation more exciting, competitors and adversaries come along too. Humans are in constant competition with each other. Mix it all up with the relationships you have with your family and friends. Your life cycle is unfolding.

Be in the same league as the elites. They know and do more right things for themselves and others. Join the positive thinkers and do-gooders who are so into it. No mountain is insurmountable. There is no such thing as bad weather; there is just bad clothing.

As long as there is wind, insects, and birds, the woods will never be silent. Settle down and listen to the cacophony of the beautiful calls of nature. Enjoy being part of the ecosystem.

Do not upset the wagon cart just because you can. Be at peace with your environment. Be innocuous. Field artillery crews often say, "What can be seen can be killed." If they cannot see you, remain hidden. Find the shoreline within yourself. Find your own watermark. Do not dwell on how you get your feet wet. Go feetfirst, headfirst, or belly flop. It is more important that you face the reality that you will swim with the current or against the current. Either way, keeping your head above water is critical.

Being vigilant is not being cowardly. At your own risk, ride the wave. You will swim or sink. If you fall asleep at the switch, you will drown. You do not have the luxury of not completely putting out the fire because it will smolder. Do not bury your head in the sand and think the hurricane will pass you by. Your buttocks may be nipped, and you might drown.

Water is refreshing in so many ways, and it is pleasing to look at a lake, a river, or an ocean. However, you do not want to be in hot water. You are in trouble if your words do not hold water. There is no pressure. Knowing your watermark and staying in balance cannot be overstated. To stay afloat, you need an anchor of solid values and trouble-management abilities. Without it, you will find yourself being tossed from one side of the water to the other for no reason.

The People You Hang Around With

The people you hang around with also make up your character. Who you hang around matters. Your companions influence your character more than you can ever imagine. It is important to pick the right group of friends. If you choose the wrong friends, you are in for a wild ride.

You need to consider some things before you choose your friends. Beware of "me, myself, and I people." They are prone to take credit for everything good, and they will blame other people for everything else. They tend to act like they are indispensable. They are often loud and hollow. Empty vessels make the most noise. Their bark is worse than their bite. The nuisance of their echo effect takes away from the order and discipline of the whole.

Plenty of these people tell lofty cock-and-bull stories and have elastic alibis. If you are the only dissenting voice or do not buy into their hoopla, you might get the cold shoulder. Be prepared to manage their wet blanket treatment. Do not be like these people. Birds of the same feather flock together.

Some people are talkers, and others are doers. It is much better to belong to the latter group. Doers always find ways to get things done. Talkers are experts at making excuses, complaining, and explaining. Are your friends mostly aligned with the microscope group or the telescope group? Do they have a positive perspective? Do they have a knack for the details? Do they have a microscope personality? Are they chasing rats while the house is on fire? The telescope characters bring distant situations nearer and make them more urgent. Choose a balanced group. Do your friends have a thermometer personality or a thermostat personality? A thermometer reads the temperature, and a thermostat regulates the temperature. Do your friends regulate your temperature like a thermostat? Are you and your friends set on the same temperature? Knowing who you hang around with will help you know who you are.

Choose friends whose personalities showcase the best of you. With the right mix of friends as your sounding board, you will stop the endless cycle of turning corners and getting dizzy. You are responsible for the friends you choose. As you become one of them, you will reap what they sow in your mind.

Reciprocity in your relationship will force you to respect the group's norms. Depending on your friends, you may join them in the bunker. Choose friends who are honorable, take care of one another, and spend time laughing with each other—not at each other.

Hang around people who uplift your spirit and not people who only see the negative in every situation. Your friends should be people who keep their word, demand honesty, and reciprocate with honesty. Listen to your inner voice. If you sense that something is off about someone, it probably is. Trust—but verify.

Do your best to pick like-minded as friends. They should add to your character. There is strength and safety in numbers. Two heads are better than one. Just be mindful that not all heads are the same.

Balance who you share your cherished secrets with. Two is a company, but three is a crowd. It is difficult to keep secrets with a crowd. Everyone has a closet and a chapter of their life they would rather keep unpublished. Be careful who you let into your most cherished thoughts. Everyone has a price. Unfortunately, weak friends can sell you out. Choose wise friends if you want to be wise. They will bring out the best of you like hot water turns tea leaves into a favorite beverage.

If you have the wrong people as friends, it will feel like chewing with a toothache. Avoid the wrong associates. They will erode your values and rob you of your sense of honor. They will siphon off your gentlemanliness, badger you, and get you to cave to the group's norms. At first, you will give in a bit, but your tolerance will gradually change to full compliance. Your compromises will grow, spread, and destroy you. As a full convert, you will beg, borrow, or steal to satisfy your need to fit in. You will become what your friends represent: the wrong crowd.

People can change. Some of your friends may be best in a certain period of your life. When your friendship has gone stale, move on. Let go of the person. Do not be a hoarder. It is important to maintain the right cycle of friendship. If you have ten problems, a bad friend should not be one of them.

You do not need a person who is always the loudest mouth in the room in your circle of friends. Some of these so-called friends may act like they have answers to all your problems, but their bodies have worse issues. Friends who do not increase you will decrease you. Avoid the doomed friends. They are bent on wiping you out.

When you run with a bad crowd, hell is bound to break loose. You will feel like a naked man who cannot put his hands in his pockets. What do you expect? After all, a cow sent to the butcher will only come out as beef. You become the next fool when you reason with fools. Hanging out with bad apples will make you a rotten character.

The product of positive ten and negative one is negative ten; the product of negative one and positive millions is negative millions. Do you get it? One negative person can alter the direction of many innocent people. Avoid bad apples. Be smart and wise. A lion leading a flock of sheep is better than a sheep leading a lion pride.

Never become a rotten character. If you do, your crimes will leave an indelible mark on you. Like a zebra, you will never be able to change your stripes. Your damaged character will be akin to your buttocks; east or west, it remains in the back. Who wants to always be at the back and lose the freedom to move ahead of the pack? Do not become a rotten character.

Bad friends are bad. People who get you to use drugs are bad friends. If you are into substance abuse or dealing, you are on your way to killing yourself. Stay away from those who want to take you to the slaughterhouse.

Smoking cigarettes is an easy habit to pick up from friends. Bad habits will cost you money, your health, and more.

When you are of drinking age, limit your alcohol intake. You can completely abstain from drinking if it suits your lifestyle. You have nothing to lose, but you will save your sanity. Never drive under the influence. If you drive drunk, you will hurt yourself and others. Driving fast is by-product of driving drunk. You lose control, and alcohol takes charge. You are on a self-appointed killing mission, and you really do not want to imagine the consequences. Before it is too late, cut ties with any so-called friends who encourage you to be an alcoholic.

Not respecting authority figures is a telltale sign of upcoming problems. Friends who encourage you to reject authority figures are bad. Once you start going down a bad road, it is very difficult to stop. Don't get into it in the first place.

Disrespecting authority figures often begins at home, but it grows wings at school and on the streets. If you sense yourself going off the trail, apply the emergency brake. Seek help from your extended family or a school counselor.

You will have problems if you and friends are involved in get-rich-quick schemes. They often border on the edge of crime. Such conduct shows deficiency in character and a lack of morals. Avoid people who try to lure you into their schemes.

If you want true glory, you must earn them. To become an Olympian, you have to be the best of the best in your country. It takes hard work, perseverance, talent, time, and maximum efforts to be competitive at that level. Success takes time. You and your friends should accept that as a fact of life.

Peer pressure can befoul good judgment. Stay alert and avoid fool's errands. To avoid setting all the wrong kinds of records, avoid being friends with those who are prone to free rides to the central lockup. Bad friends come with a prize.

If you choose to hang around folks who break the law, you are cementing your character. Don't be a lawbreaker. If you do the crime, be ready to do the time. Breaking the law may result in prison time. In prison, your life will reach a significant crossroads. Don't let your freedom be taken. Prison will kick you where it hurts. It will make you feel like a caged animal. You will feel like you have lost everything, including your dignity. You will hear stories about crimes by other inmates that will dwarf yours. You will quickly learn who the boss is. They are the big dogs, and you are the small dog. You will need to watch your back. I've never heard of anyone liking life in the brig. Who could forget being under the microscope and under the total control of the prison staff?

Prison will give you time to reflect on whether you are a professional criminal or an amateur. It will force you to pause, doubt yourself, and assess your life. Violence begets violence.

Being locked up would bring grief to your family. Do not choose a life of crime.

Prison will give you time to search your soul for your better angels. You may see your condition as temporary. You are down, but you are not hopeless. You might try to repent from your ways, find your new self, and find God when you are free again. You might learn from the criminals and be worse when you are released back into the society. You might learn the hard way. You might learn the hard truth.

Recidivism rates increase after being locked up a few times. You are likely to find yourself going in and out of jail. Try to avoid being a repeat offender; one incarceration is enough to set off a domino effect that can derail your life goals.

If you have learned your lessons doing time, you will avoid walking on thin ice in the future. Taking the path of least resistance is not an accident; it is the choice you make.

Mixing water and electricity is fatal. Avoid making bad choices and having bad friends. They could open the door to your demise. If you are on the wrong side of the law, you could end up in a cemetery or a prison. Stay clean, avoid precarious situations, and live honorably. Make it your character to be friends with people who share your values.

◆ ◆ ◆

In life, the splinters will occasionally point toward you. If you have been righteously building honorable character, you will dig deep and draw from your character reservoir, values, trouble-management skills, and lessons from hanging out with the right people. You will know the best time to take a leap of faith. When the smoke clears, you will see the character you developed over the years.

At the end of the day, you should not be scared of your own shadow. If your shadow spooks you, something is wrong. Your character may be flawed. With a flawed character, you are more likely to go adrift and get lost in life. You could be in a closed loop with no beginning and no ending. The feeling will be like a spear being thrust into your chest. If you pull out the spear, you will bleed to death. If you leave the spear in place, you are bound for a slow death from the internal damage.

Build an honorable character early in life. Hold values that foster doing things the right way. Effectively and efficiently manage your life troubles. Since iron sharpens iron, hang around with honorable characters.

CHAPTER 5

EDUCATION

GG says education is life's cornerstone; get it right. The first draft of your education is natural, and it starts at birth. It requires parental guidance and nurturing.

Your second draft should address your formal schooling—kindergarten through post-high school education.

The third and last draft incorporates your daily experiences and lessons learned in the trenches of life. Altogether, here is your educational outlook.

If you are the type of person who cares about what is behind door one, two, or three, you will tend to want to learn more. And if you know more, you will have more options to do more with what you have learned.

As a kid, your parents are the center beam for your total well-being. Your parents' unspecified responsibility includes getting you educated. All things being equal, your parents should provide conducive environment for you to live and learn. Your parents model behavior that will go a long way toward educating you. There is nothing like parents' strong words and stronger actions.

You will never forget your parents' words about education. You will never forget your parents telling you that you will be somebody someday. They told you to study to be a doctor or a lawyer. Parents inspire their kids. They give them hope with their candid talk. If you do the right things, tomorrow will turn out better. If you listen and do as you are told and get your education, you can expect a bright future. You will never regret it.

From kindergarten through high school, many kids from poor neighborhoods face challenges that cannot even be imagined by kids from well-off neighborhoods. Being hungry or not having enough to eat are things poor kids know too well. Putting on whatever clothes and shoes are available is a pattern they know too well. They ask for school fees and expenses while being fully aware that their parents have no money to give. That is another gut-wrenching experience.

In their homes, the living spaces can be a challenge. Many poor kids share a room with multiple people. There is no claiming a space for themselves, which means distractions during study time and more. These kids may not have a support structure that promotes academic excellence. Walking and seeing kids off to or from school sounds like a luxury for a lot them. One of many reasons is the parents' work hours. Nefarious reasons could also be a factor.

Bad home situations force some of these kids to be self-reliant very early in life, and they have to act like adults. Although they are still kids, their character will be tested like adults. Some will succumb to the glamour of street life. Their educations will suffer.

For many underprivileged kids, school is an oasis in the desert of life. School equips them with living tools. It rekindles and keeps their spark on. School instills hope and serves as their agent of last resort.

Despite the realities of their situations and the stumbling blocks along the way, many of these kids work hard and persevere.

They are deservedly proud when they beat the odds and earn a high school diploma. For those who pursue higher education, the next step should not be an accident. The foundation of education is laid way before high school graduation. Good grades in high school are the starting point. Using the four-point scale, a high grade point average of three or above speaks positively about the student. Participation in sports and athletic events will boost your rating. Leadership roles in extracurricular activities will enhance your rating.

Investing in tutorials for college entrance tests—ACT or SAT—is worth the extra points. Of course, keep a target score and specific college requirements in mind. When all is put together, using the whole person concept, you will have a leg up during the college admission process.

The big elephant in the room is the cost of attending college. *Behemoth* and *intimidating* are a few words to describe the common feeling when you lack resources. Tuition, fees, boarding, and books cost tens of thousands of dollars per year. When you add transportation, clothing, and other personal expenses, an in-state student can easily burn twenty-five thousand dollars. Imagine the burden this places on a poor student. You do not want to know. Sadly, there is no government program coming to the rescue. Grants are partial. Existing loan programs tether poor students to many years of loan repayments.

Many poor kids need scholarships if their college dreams come true without massive debt anchoring them down and thwarting their chances of living life free of debt. Academic scholarships enable some to get college degrees. Sports have provided a gateway for few. Military academy and Reserve Officers' Training Corps programs are used by some. Many more should commit to serving their country. The rewards are immense.

If you have a moderate means or humble beginnings, start early in school and work smarter to secure the financial assistance to help fund college. Your goal should be to complete your college degree with little or no debt. When you keep more of your income, you can build wealth faster and join the middle class or the upper middle class. You will gain a lot from being educated. Education will spark and fuel your curiosity about how things work. Education will give you the building blocks to go beyond being a spectator. You will start being a participant. Education will increase your social, emotional, intelligence, and adversity quotients, which leads to a balanced life. Education will equip you with guardrails for life. It will help pave the way to more learning. It will help you to be good today and better tomorrow. It will help you imagine or relive eureka moments.

When you start working on your education early and want it bad enough, you are more likely to get it than not. Give your education the seriousness it deserves. To survive your education odyssey, keep your hands on the steering wheel. The rewards will be worth all the effort. The best mountain views come to those that climb. When you are on top of the mountain, you will see the plains. You need a structured education and unstructured learning to get to the mountaintop. You can join the parade of champions.

CHAPTER 6

LEARNING

According to GG, you should know a little about everything. The more you know, the more interesting you are. After high school diplomas and college degrees are the uncertificated but very important life lessons. This part includes your everyday experiences. These experiences will sharpen your field acuity. They will manifest themselves in your interactions with people and the things in the world.

Have you ever wondered if your academic achievements can guarantee you success in life? They rarely do. Your daily actions and reactions will catapult or derail your success more than any institutional training you have. Apply what you know in a manner that make you a welcomed member of the team.

To be successful, you must know a lot about something and be good at it. Do you need to be an expert? Maybe, maybe not. When you know a lot about many things—but are a master of none—you are a generalist. You will demonstrate different degrees of knowledge on matters at hand and draw from your subject matter expert and generalist hats to meet life's demands. If you do well, your confidence will rise. If you flop due to a lack of knowledge, you will feel like a deflated balloon.

To continue to improve, learn more, practice more, and rehearse more. Knowledge will unlock a boundless imagination for a caged mind. You will be the beneficiary. Your mind is fertile ground. It is just waiting to be plowed, seeded, watered, bloomed, and harvested. Use your mind. Do not leave it in dormant state for long. Learn and gain knowledge. It is power.

Once you are a learned person, your knowledge will affect the way you look at things—and the things you look at will change. Your knowledge will widen your aperture and make you smarter about the information you consume. You will take in information with a grain of salt. You will not overthink situations, and you will avoid being overly cautious and missing opportunities. Numbers only tell half the story because there are always extenuating contexts.

Learning will help you avoid ignorance and help you mitigate unforced crises. It will open up new possibilities and make you ready when opportunity knocks. Once you have acquired the relevant knowledge, you will emerge like a star that has been continuously shining—but only noticed in the dark.

There will be learning opportunities everywhere. When you read, you change. When you travel, you change. When you listen to people, you change. When you attend social events and mix with people, you change. Songs change across generations. Writing styles and colloquialisms change in syntax and semantics with time. Social norms evolve. Life changes are as certain as knowing night will fall and daylight will follow. There are great learning moments for you to discover around every corner.

As you learn new things, you will also have opportunities to unlearn your bad experiences.

Life is linear path, but it is full of unexpected randomness. You can look at the mystery through the prism of your personal perceptions. If you learn and practice as much as magicians do, you will feel a seamlessness in your life. Learning will help you extrapolate between the past, present, and future. The more knowledge you acquire, the more intellectual you will be.

Your life is the sum of your daily actions. By acting productively daily, you will achieve a greater outcome. Your life does not operate in a vacuum; you are a part of your life equation.

As soon as you realize everywhere is a classroom, you will be more alert. Keep your antenna up for new information that will enrich your life. Always learn something from the people in front of you. Problems are part of life's education curriculum. Some of the lessons you learn will last a lifetime, and others will fade away quickly. Be mindful of the noise interference.

Keep learning. Do not leave your brain idle; that is the devil's workshop. Your brain is not furniture that decorates your skull. It is your intellectual powerhouse. If you use it properly, you will be rewarded handsomely. Feed your brain. A healthy brain is actively gaining wisdom and solving complex problems. Use your brain for good.

Learn from anyone, and value anyone who touches you. Reading other people's experiences will give you access to information and lessons, which will reduce your trial-and-error rate and improve your chances for success.

Do not forget to ask for help. Everyone needs help at one point or another. Seek counsel from qualified people. Ask the coaches, mentors, and wise people around you. The wisdom they offer may be critical to your survival. You will live to fight another day.

Society has norms and ground rules. Find out what they are and know them, but do not hold to dated ideas that make you forget that time passes and things change.

Situations may be similar, but their conditions and contexts are rarely the same. Things change as time passes. Skills and knowledge are constantly updated. What used to be peculiar to only one culture can become universal practice in other cultures. Rap music is a good example. Dress styles, leather coats, and fries and burgers are other examples. Grammar rules change. Transportation modes evolve from horse-drawn carriages to unmanned aerial vehicles. The digital revolution has changed the modern information landscape. The industrial age has been reworked into a more robotic era with artificial intelligence. Old jobs like coal mining are losing ground, and the gig economy is emerging.

Change is here, and the art of change is constant. Learn to embrace and adapt to the new ways or risk losing your relevancy. If you want to see the sun rise, look east and not west. Dial back and forth if you are interested in seeing the sun set in the west and not the east.

We have to coexist with others in our society. Be socially aware. Note what is said and not said. Read between the lines. Learn something from them or about them. Be alert. Be an active learner. Recognize your place and the hour—and be glad in it. You are ready when you know you are in the right place at the right time.

Make your presence known. Vote with your heart, money, and feet. Act on what you agree on. Negotiate on what you disagree on. Do not cling to old ways. Adjust and upgrade your skills to stay in line with the times you live in and the days ahead.

The world is changing every day. Figure out where you are in the change cycle and adapt. We are citizens of the digital age. Stay internet smart or be left behind. Know where you are in the continuum of where you are going. Actively seek to stay current and relevant in your life. Be prepared to anchor yourself during storms and resume your journey when the storm passes.

What do you read? Make it a point to start a reading list with the best authors in different genres. Read the classics: George Orwell (*Animal Farm*); Chinua Achebe (*Things Fall Apart*); William Shakespeare (*Julius Caesar*), and Homer (*The Odyssey*). Check out books by Agatha Christy (*Death on the Nile*) and Arthur Conan Doyle (*Sherlock Holmes*). Research different genres for renowned authors (old and new) and read their best works. These authors are reputable for a reason. Read their works and discover the intrigue.

Consider reading books from the four main literary genres (nonfiction, fiction, drama, and poetry. Take your pick from a range of book options: children, young adult, folktale, science, autobiographies, biographies and memoirs, crime, thrillers, horror, romance, inspirational, Bible, spiritual, military, self-help, and how-to books. Your goal should be to read one to three books a month, depending on the book type, size, and ease of read.

Make time to gradually and methodically read the Bible; it is the most consequential and richest book for Christians. Autobiographies, biographies, and memoirs of successful people (athletes, entrepreneurs, leaders, educators, and professionals of different stripes) give you the total package.

Mix up your reading list to spice things up and acquire a balance of knowledge. If you devour books from the best writers, you will find nuggets of wisdom in unexpected places. By the time you have leisurely gone through three hundred books from diverse genres, you will fall in love with certain authors and writing styles.

It is blissful when you start savoring the energy and effort put in by the authors to bring the books to life. Their choice of words, strings of words, and wordplay will leave an imprint on you. Some plots and characters will keep you in suspense and make your imagination run wild. Some will provide insights or solutions. Some will be laced with action-packed adventures. Some are straight-out entertaining. Some are informative, and some engage and challenge your curiosity. Yes, different authors have different flavors.

By reading the books, you will learn about the authors' ideas and lifestyles. You will learn to put on your own oxygen mask before lending a hand to the person next to you. You will do something for somebody other than yourself. You will learn that you need mentors or coaches who will observe, instruct, and inspire you. When the going gets tough, successful people do not go internal and wallow in self-pity. Instead, they doggedly hang in there like professional bull riders who do their best during the eight-second ride. Of course, the bull always wins.

You will appreciate all of this and more, including their writing styles and how the authors evolved over the years. Iconic books have earned their reputations. If you pay attention, your awareness of the new trends in writing will emerge. The more you read, the more you know—and the more you appreciate learning.

As long as your intellectual curiosity remains aflame, the joy of reading will be fulfilling. Reading is an investment in your brain, and the return on that investment is unmatched. Books will take you to places you have never been. Books will expand your thinking. Books will sharpen your mind with the possibilities seen in the characters you read. Books will increase your vocabulary, and effective word selection comes from reading good books. Reading will rub off on your fine-tuned sentence structure, enhance your speaking eloquence, and affect your word selection and sentence construction.

When you read the best books, you will get hooked into being a lifelong reader. You will come across as smart and educated, which may translate into above-average earning power. Well-read people tend to have more confidence. Who wants to pass up on that? If you read the best books, you have a better chance of being one of the best.

Think about how you wish to be remembered. Keep your eyes on the prize. Where you spend your time and energy—and where you do not—speaks to your values and interests. Learning will help open your eyes to who you are and who you hope to be. At your leisure, revisit important subjects from elementary school because they are part of your learning foundation and might need reinforcement.

Elementary mathematics (addition, subtraction, multiplication, and division and statistics, geometry, and simple algebra) will help with your abstract thinking. Elementary social sciences (history, geography, and economics) will enhance your reference points in life. General sciences (biology, chemistry, and physics) will help you decode things that would otherwise remain mysteries. At a minimum, skim through the elementary subjects online. You will be surprised by how much you can recollect and reinforce what you know.

If you did not listen to your elementary school teachers, you may be behind the eight ball. Your learning progression may be stunted. You may need to do some catch-up reading or continue to suffer from a lack of knowledge. Higher education builds on elementary subjects, and the basics remain the same. At a minimum, know the geography of your state, country, and continent. Be familiar with the basic elementary school subjects. Knowing just enough about these important subjects can make you dangerous as you reach and draw from your knowledge reservoir during your interactions with others.

In daily living, generalists excel because they know a lot about many things. If you are still in elementary school, pay attention. Ask questions when you are confused or lost. Do not let peer pressure hold you back. Most of your peers have the same questions in mind. Most will be happy that someone asked the question. Do not be an interruptive student who asks questions they already know the answers to.

You can ask your teachers for explanations. Good teachers love students who want to learn. The students who understood the training may be able to explain the topic. Make it a point to ask for help before the lesson moves on to the next steps. Since classes build on prior lessons, never allow yourself to fall behind. Like swimming or riding a bike, once you have the hang of it, you can swim or ride for fun. Try to like all your elementary school subjects. Try to learn because your life really depends on them.

Disregard discouraging words. Don't listen when people say, "You can't be good at anything." Hell no! You are somebody, and you will be something.

Learn to be comfortable in your own skin. Even if you made a mess at the onset, failure is not a permanent condition. If you fail twice, bounce back thrice. You will be whatever you want to be. Your destiny is in your hands. Working smarter and doing the right things always pays off.

◆ ◆ ◆

Learning a language other than your native tongue will give you an edge in life. If you are a native English speaker, adopt a second language. Take your pick from the world's most spoken languages: Spanish, Mandarin, French, Arabic, or African dialects. The ability to understand and speak a foreign tongue is a priceless asset.

Imagine the wow factor and the facial expressions when they realize you have understood them all along. It can be a funny predicament. Depending on what was said, your hosts might feel betrayed, embarrassed, or happy that you can see things from their viewpoint. You won't need an interpreter because you can relate to them. A familiarity with your adopted language will endear you to the people and make it easier to assimilate into your hosts' community.

Being bilingual keeps your brain more active as you switch between languages. While your native tongue comes naturally, your second tongue may task your brain a bit more. No worries. If you start early in learning a second language, it will soon be second nature. You will be able to communicate effortlessly. To speak multiple languages on autopilot is cool as a cucumber. You will enjoy the sense of pride that comes with being a gifted speaker of a second language. Of course, the second language will enable you to reach out to native speakers, make friends more quickly, and be accepted faster.

If being appreciated is one of your top desires, being bilingual paves the way. Many employers will pay extra to have a bilingual staff.

Traveling to new places will let you see things you have never seen before. Be open-minded and enjoy it. Your lessons will never end. You will be amazed at the different greetings and foods. Focus on what matters instead of the politics. Do not be pigeonholed. Be ready for change without surrendering your principles. Life is like assembling a jigsaw puzzle without picture—everything is amenable to learning and working hard.

◆ ◆ ◆

You came into the world without any blueprint for how to make it through the wilderness of life. The goal should be to live like you will die tomorrow and learn like you will live forever. Asking the right questions will get you better responses. Putting the knowledge you acquired along your journey into practice will enhance the quality of your life. Continue learning and practicing.

Music is complex and tells its own stories. Music is universal language, and it is a good learning tool for understanding what the singers are thinking. Music is generational, and it transcends cultural boundaries. When you appreciate incredible works of the art, you will be in a position to dissect the different instruments and beats.

You can learn a lot from lyrics. Take these in and reflect on them: "I'll Always Love You" by Whitney Houston, "Ballad of the Green Berets" by Barry Sadler, "Bad Reputation" by Joan Jett, "Fast Car" by Tracy Chapman, "Many Rivers to Cross" by Jimmy Cliff, "Changes" by Tupac Shakur, "I'll Do Anything for Love" by Meatloaf, "If I Could Turn Back Time" by Cher, and "The Gambler" by Kenny Rogers.

Do not forget the dance moves that go along with the music. There is a lot to gain from listening to good music, particularly ones with international recognition. Music will definitely get you into a party mood. Make music a part of your relaxing menu and learning repertoire. By extension, respecting specialties in various walks of life will stimulate your interest in knowing more about them. You can learn a ton by paying attention to people who excel in their crafts and trades.

Watch animals and birds in the wild or at least on TV. Programs about ocean and space exploration will open your eyes about the universe we live in. Your appreciation for the ecosystem will change for good. Learn from nature. It is interesting to know that wild animals run from something or toward something. They live in an environment or ecosystem where predators kill at will. Innocence is not a pass to safety. Pecking order fights can easily turn fatal. Strong lions thrive until they are dethroned or banished by up-and-coming heirs.

Compared to wild animals, human life is not that hard. Instead, the obstacles you face give you opportunities to learn more about yourself. And if there is a warning, it means someone did something. The tyranny of averages could affect the statistics of the good folks in your community.

◆ ◆ ◆

No matter what, retain a zest for learning, get better, and learn to make the world a better place for all. Today, the news spews twenty-four-seven into people's lives. Some people go out of their way to be the news. Always being a news maker tends to get into a news maker's head.

Most people's sources of news will tell their political leaning: liberal or conservative. Even revealing a person's regular news source can elicit bias on an issue. It is best not to limit your news consumption to one particular viewpoint. It is good to hear opposing views too. Balanced information leads to balanced knowledge.

Add independent news outlets to your news consumption menu. Complement your news intake with subscriptions to business, professional, and industry magazines. Tons of newsletters, blogs, webcasts, and press releases are available to be dumped into your email inbox every day. Most subscriptions are free.

Newsfeeds from social media platforms are here to stay. Subscribe to TedTalks for specialty insights and speeches. With an open mind, peruse them all. You will learn one or two things, and you will be glad you did. At the end of the day, you will be better informed and have balanced knowledge. The key is maximum exposure.

There are no absolutes in life. If you pay attention, you will notice that ideologies overlap. Make an effort to know more about the whole. Do not just dig into your narrow silo and think the world revolves around you. It does not. You live in an interdependent world. Other people have a right to be where they are. Know that—and act like you do. Learn to know what right looks like.

Is it OK to deride a fat person or a little person? Is it OK to disrespect others? Is it OK to thumb your nose at the Ten Commandments when keeping them is not your choice? The better angel inside you tells you not to hurt others, but you disregard that heavenly voice. You choose to dehumanize others for their gender, age, race, color, religion, disability, or national origin, and you forget that these people have feelings too. Wrong is wrong. Treat others as you want to be treated.

You may borrow few elements of the US Army's values (respect, integrity, personal courage, and honor) to buttress your moral anchor. Your honor is priceless. If you lose it, your reputation is gone. Your reputation is your character.

Program yourself to look for what is right and decide what is right. Check when you are more negative than positive. Find twice as many good things as bad things. Learn to self-correct.

Words can hurt. Do not put a dagger in other people's souls with your words. Watch what you say. Rain can wash away footprints, but words can simmer deep into the soul. Only the victim can give permission to heal the damage. Once hurtful words are discharged, you cannot recall them and get things back to normal. It's like trying to put the toothpaste back in the tube.

When you mess up, accept that you are wrong. It takes courage. Apologize sincerely. Tear up if you will. Do not be a stone. Even stones make noise when they are smashed by ocean waves or blasted by wind. Do not be a person with no emotions. Being emotionless is not a strength. Being contrite and asking for forgiveness will give you a better chance of being forgiven.

Learn to put yourself in others' shoes and empathize with them. Do not dwell on other people being in your shoes. Do not act like a victim. You will be disappointed. Many individuals only view life through the distortion prism of their fortunes or misfortunes, and they barely think others could be experiencing worse situations.

There is always something to learn from the best or worst of humanity. Copy the good and discard the bad relics of bygone eras. Draw insights from what you learn. Do not leave common sense at the door. Adapt to the world around you. You will win some and lose some, but you will live to fight another day.

Adversity will show up at your doorstep. Knowing and avoiding conflict triggers, hot buttons, and flared emotion are good tactics. Open and honest discussions are important for seeing how the other people see issues. Most people care about respect and fairness.

The path to being amiable is fraught with difficulty, but you can anchor yourself to a biblical saying: "Ask and you will receive, seek and you will find, and knock and the door will be opened." Believe you can have healthy relationships with others because you can.

Until the lion tells his story, the story of the hunt belongs to the hunter. Allow others to tell their stories and learn to persuade others to listen to you telling your own story in your own way. Emulate the greatest of all time in whatever walk of life you find your passion. Look at Martin Luther King Jr. if nonviolence is your fancy. Look at Pele if soccer is your call. Warren Buffet, Carlos Kleiber, and Napoleon Bonaparte all provide life trails to follow.

Put your signature on what you have learned and own it. Society tends to gravitate toward people who know stuff. Like smoke, people who know stuff find a way to rise to the occasion. They end up leading the pack. You can be one of the people who know stuff. When you learn, you evolve personally and professionally. One day, you may be the man of the hour.

Growth is a factor in your life journey. You will either grow or die. Identify your goal and apply yourself in preparation for the golden hour. No human condition is permanent; everything is transitory until the day we check out of life.

Life is a school. Continue to learn as much as you can. Know a little about everything. Understand that everything has season. You may not remember everything you learned, but the lessons from your failures and successes will remain fresh in your mind.

Beware of the tyranny of the majority and systemic thinking. Learn from every situation. Learn what to do and what not to do. There are always lessons to harness in any experience. Jot down new findings as they sneak into your cognitive sphere. The new knowledge may slip out or be overtaken by the competing events if it is not timely captured. Immortalize the new lessons. Review your notes periodically. Your brain will absorb the information and convert it into bytes. The value of good ideas is nominal until they are put into practice. That is where they count the most. Your everyday experiences will strengthen your ability to knit together ideas and become an expert in your area of interest. Many drops of water make an ocean.

Eventually, your web of experience—including your book smarts, your street smarts, and your people smarts—will propel you to be the master of your destiny. The generations that come after you can learn from your success.

Learn to give to others. It is easier to take from others than to give, but kinder hearts find it more soothing to give than to take. Giving back will make your family, your community, and the world a better place.

CHAPTER 7

BELIEF IN GOD

GG says faith in God is empowering. Believe in God. Fear of the Lord is the beginning of wisdom. He gives us life, and no miracle is greater than life. Have faith in Him. He will never forsake you. One person with God constitutes a majority.

When you wake up in the morning, be positive. Say, "I'm grateful. Lord, please lead the way." Go out into the world and be a blessing for someone. Thank God at the end of each day. Have your plan for the next day before you go to sleep.

Peace comes when you know God is in charge. You will have no problems living simply, loving generously, and leaving things that are beyond your control to God. You will not allow pride, greed, or anger to overtake you or destroy you. Your values and character inside and out will showcase your love of God.

When your inside is right—at peace—your outside will be right too. Why not join the fellowship of other believers in praising and glorifying God? Yes, a church is a house of worship. Go to church and enjoy fellowship with other believers.

Good church worship is uplifting. You will feel like you are part of a force of nature. Most of your worries will take a backseat as you are engulfed in the warmth of praising and glorifying the heavenly Father. It is an experience worth having even for a short time. Do you have mixed feelings about going to church? You are not alone. Do churchgoers' lives dissuade you? Be clear-eyed. Put your faith in God and not man.

Walking into a church to be a member will cost you. You will feel the weight of constant pleas for money. It is common to see sermons punctuated with fundraising themes, which dilute the true messages.

Personal interest in amassing worldly materials and living in comfort make many people sacrifice their morals. Due to human frailties and vulnerabilities, during trial and tribulations, many people fall short in following the Bible. To cover up their flaws, some lift biblical quotes and use them out of context to justify their devious deeds. Cherry-picking and interpreting verses in the Bible to suit conceited ways is wrong.

Many people do unspeakable deeds to circumvent biblical teachings. They violate the biblical scriptures with reckless abandon. They gross over or pay lip service to the words. They pick and choose the ones that support their ulterior motives and agendas. Sadly, as these flaws are repeated, the population becomes numb to them. Fewer people raise their eyebrows as a sign of resentment. Every day that passes, these bad ways are tolerated more or even accepted.

As a result of the unexemplary lives lived by some preachers and parishioners—whose daily lifestyle is anathema to what they preach to the public—many congregants and would-be congregants question their faith.

Try not to let the actions of the bad actors deter you from loving God with all your heart. Do right in your private life—even if you elect not to go to church.

Converts and non-coverts have the right to doubt if there is a true God. The mystery is that God is omnipresent, omniscient, and omnipotent. As human beings, we are given the intelligence to question whatever our senses perceive. It is no crime to be inquisitive, particularly about the Bible and God. If you lack faith, God lends Himself to whatever interpretation you elect. Unfortunately, some so-called God-fearing people exploit the parables and obfuscate biblical teachings to align with their ungodly agendas. If you are a true believer in God, take the Bible as gospel truth and live the words as humanly as possible.

Beware of the zillions of false preachers in every nook and corner of your community. They profess to have a special pass to God that their congregation lacks. They do magic to impress. They see visions and prophesize about a future that never comes true. They want your money by hook or by crook. None of these conceited acts are new. Do not let the crooked Bible-toting false men or women of God turn you into a brainwashed puppy. If it looks like a scam, it is a scam. Run.

It does take money to run a church. Support it wisely. Give what you can afford, but do not go into debt because of your church. Give because you care about their mission and what they actually do.

◆　◆　◆

Have you ever thought about the different religions of the world? They appear to be geographically centered and time-stamped. What if all these religions were true pathways to God? If people know it and accept it, that could eliminate the religious feuds we experience.

Most of the world's population belongs to the dominant religions: Christianity, Islam, Hinduism, Buddhism, Sikhism, and Judaism. These religions, in one form or another, hold spiritual beliefs with varying interpretations of the gateway to God. They all worship God in their own ways.

Why the difference in religions? The key seems to be the various interpretations and relative importance of their origins and any disagreements as they evolve. The separating factors in the dominant religions include types of institutions and sacred places; rites and rituals; leaders and vested authorities; society and geographical locations; beliefs rooted in strict cultural and spiritual teachings; puritanical ideologies; and afterlife outlooks. Within religions, internal divisions exist. There are different denominations and sects. Christianity has Catholic, Protestant, and Orthodox factions. Digging deeper, you will see further subdivisions and subsets. No wonder no religion can boast absolute homogeneity.

Other than the followers of the dominant religions, some people have no religion. Atheists and agnostics subscribe to the idea of no Supreme Being. Some people practice indigenous or ethnic religions. Their practices and traditions are location specific. These people are considered pagans, heathens, or animists. They worship nature and the cosmos for supernatural powers. They see ancestors and immortals as mediums to the Supreme Being. They have deities, and they are in awe of them.

Due to believers living side by side, some religious teachings bleed over, which leads to changes. This is a contributing factor for making what was normal at a certain period into something abnormal in another period. Religions soften and harden with time.

Religious affiliations tend to be geographically dependent. Your region, country, or continent can provide indicators of your religious affiliation. Yes, every part of the world has prevailing religions. Your geography will determine your religious doctrine exposure or lack thereof. If you are born on an island, your chance of being a swimmer are good. If you are born into a religion, the chances you will remain in it are high. Of course, some people adopt new religions, and some people drop religion. Gaining and losing converts between religions or factions seems to be a historical pattern.

Your religious affiliation is mostly an accident of chance, but it leaves room for individuals to select an unpopular religion.

Every religion sees itself as the only way to God. This can stir cultural clashes and foster religious intolerance, rivalries, and disunity. What if a heterogeneous religion was there to suit all the regions of the world?

The most important thing should not be your religion. The important thing should be whether you are a good person to yourself and others. Do you treat others as you want to be treated? You owe it to yourself and the world to avoid religious feuds. Be tolerant and be good to others.

In religion, there is your side of the story, their side, and the truth. God is the truth. And God welcomes all. There is God. If you still doubt that, think about the last time you were in a do-or-die situation. What flashed through your mind? Did you ask God to help you? The request appeared to be triggered subconsciously. You may not have thought about God until that moment of dire need. Why do we invoke God's name in our bleakest moments?

In near-death experiences, something inside you yields your existence to something mightier than yourself: God. People who survived near-death experiences have reported sightings of heavenly phenomena. What if you rejected God now and have to meet Him at the end of your earthly journey? Imagine your feelings. It would be worse than going to beg your archenemy for a blood transfusion to save your life.

Hey, believe in God now. What do you have to lose?

Understand how God works. Have faith and ask God to come into your life. Ask God for things that are beyond your control. Bear your own cross first, do not ask for material riches, and watch the miracles happen.

If you are asking God to see the African folklore story of a turtle climbing a rope, you may be waiting until eternity to see that. Be practical and contextual. There's no need to try your God. God created life, and no miracle is greater than life. Take a moment to think about the ingenuity of how your body works. God made you.

◆ ◆ ◆

Own a Bible. Read it regularly. You can diligently read it from cover to cover and boast about it to your friends. Put in an honest effort to understand the teachings as they are written. Do not skew the true meaning of the verses for your convenience or benefit your ungodly ways. Abide by God's Word as much as possible.

The younger you are and the earlier you immerse yourself into Godly ways, the more your life will be grounded in pure ideals and holiness. Be the light nonbelievers see, have a change of heart, and accept Christ as the Son of God.

There is a phenomenal value about truly believing in God. When you find yourself overwhelmed, pray and hand your burden to God. The quickest way out of fear is to believe in God. Believing that God will answer your prayers is empowering. Accepting that God's wishes will be done should lighten your burden. Have faith. God is with you. Do you feel better?

Without the biblical metrics, how would you measure your moral compliance or deficiency? Are you listening to God's voice or evil's voice in your head? It is subjective.

Why forgo the Ten Commandments and Christ's teachings, which offer a guide for moral living? It is your choice to stray from them and make straight lines crooked. It is your choice to allow wrong to triumph over right. It is your choice to be on God's side. God is worth your time.

Give your life to God or to the devil. You can choose to go beyond the binary options and make it complicated by throwing in gray areas. You quibble when you argue that a broken clock is right twice every day. You may shackle yourself with contrarian values. That is why the perfect condition to serve God is elusive. Believing in the biblical teachings will help you stay anchored to God's ways and avoid going down the road to nowhere.

Jesus, God's Son, went through trials and tribulations, criticism, death, and resurrection. Do not be overly critical or judgmental of yourself. Be the best you. Honoring with the lips and not by the heart is hypocrisy. No matter the trials and tribulations, never be ashamed of believing in God.

There is no free lunch. Everything has a cost—even your faith in God. People may prosecute you. Always come to God to thank Him, praise Him, and give Him your worries.

Do to others as you would want others to do to you. That is one of the cardinal pronouncements in the Bible. Why are believers all over the world not absolutely onboard in loving their neighbors and treating them as they would want to be treated? That is hypocrisy.

Faith in God will make you reevaluate your life and your purpose. Faith is the cornerstone to God being the source of miracles. Early in the morning and before bedtime, give your worries and praises to God. Doing so will help you put things into perspective. Accept that God's decision cannot be appealed.

Man proposes, but God disposes. Walk by your faith, and then use your sight as a backup. The Bible is simple, but some people's interpretations make it confusing. Do not shortchange the Word of God.

Once you put on your oxygen mask, help your neighbor. Do not give oxygen to evil deeds. Right is right—even if everyone is against it. God is not tempting you to do wrong; Satan is. Always ask God for courage to do the right things.

Do not pray for a tornado to befall your enemy and blow the person into oblivion. Instead, be dangerous to the devil by being a blessing to others. Overcome evil with good. The Bible is a repository of knowledge, truth, and wisdom that serves as a beacon to life with morality. Reading the Bible nourishes the soul, and abiding by the Word of God enriches your happiness.

Beware of implicit or unconscious bias in race, ethnicity, gender, or human condition. Everyone has it. If you love God, celebrate people. They are His creation. Be kind to everyone. Welcome others with a genuine smile and care. If Jesus Christ were in your neighborhood today, would you recognize, respect, and approve of Him?

The lessons from the Bible are timeless. The Bible showcases a lot of characters, and studying them will be rewarding: Sarah (faith), David (courage), Solomon (wisdom), Rehoboam (counsel), and Paul (repentance). Each of them tells a captivating story.

Make God priority one, family priority two, and work priority three. Put your faith in God—and then prepare to take off.

Help improve the lives of other people and the systems they live under. Extend your arms and heart to your neighbors. A rubber band is most useful when it's stretched. Find someone in need, do something to help that person, and pass forward your blessings.

When you serve others, life is meaningful because you are living with a greater purpose than yourself. Your soul is enriched, and it abounds with happiness. You may only help a fraction of the people who need help, but be proud that you are touching the ones you did and making a difference. Do more than hand out—lend a hand.

When you do good for others, you feel good. When you feel good, you are warmer. Without a spiritual anchor, you are hollow inside and maybe devoid of happiness.

Believing in God Almighty will help you focus on what is important. Being faithful as the Bible espouses will help you conquer fear that defies logic. You will sleep tight because God got your six.

Immoral acts are evil and unnecessary. Illegal acts are forbidden. Unethical acts are crooked and unnecessary. Once your inner compass is calibrated to always do what is right, you are on your way to spiritual wellness.

Operate within the realms of your sanity and not your vanity. If you live life full of vanity, your spiritual well-being will be like seeds on stony ground or thorny weeds. If sanity dominates your ways, you are likely to yield great fruits like seeds on good ground. Be prepared for the coming of our Lord, Jesus Christ.

Do God's work now—in any way you know. Go to church and have fellowship with fellow believers. Use your life camera to capture scenes you like and those you do not like, and then print the pictures or delete them. Put yourself in front of the line, on the inside track, and be a light in the dark.

Refuse to be silence whenever and wherever people are oppressed. Speak up against merchants of deceit and discord. On behalf of God, be the person watching the watchman. Physical inspection means little if the inside makeup is not examined. The greatest mistake is doing nothing.

Anything can happen in a split second. Accidents can happen to anybody—good and bad people included. You can lose everything in an accident. Things happen. People get kicked in the teeth. Even notable people fall from grace to grass. A hero can go to a zero in very short order. Such is life. It behooves you to be prepared to meet the Lord whenever He calls.

What if the end is not the end? Imagine living in paradise with God or being cast to hell with Satan. If believing in Jesus to get the eternal blessing, grace, joy, and peace is not your thing, how else can you get there?

CHAPTER 8

HEALTH

GG says everyone welcomes the idea of being healthy, but when told what it takes to be healthy, many clam up and turn into passive shells. Your health deserves your undivided attention because good health is one of your most prized possessions. Your genetics, environment, and lifestyle impact your health. You have to live with your genes—whether you like it or not—but you have a bit of control over your environment and lifestyle.

If you are born with genetically predisposed conditions, accept it and seek medical treatment if necessary. Spiritual salvation should be a backup. Under the watchful eyes of medical professionals, manage your expectations and align them with realities.

Live a life that makes sense. Make your hay while the sun is shining. Once you recognize you are in an unhealthy environment, make a point to get out of it as soon as it is feasible. Head for greener pastures. A healthy environment will help you improve your conditions, manage your genetically predisposed outcomes, and build a healthy lifestyle.

Diet and exercise are elements of a healthy lifestyle. You are what you eat. If your daily food intake (calories) is a lot greater than your burn rate, expect to become overweight sooner than later.

The type of food you eat and the portion size matter. A good rule of thumb for a healthy plate is half vegetable, one-quarter proteins, and one-quarter carbohydrates. Eat more high-fiber foods—fruits and vegetables—because they make you full faster. If you can, add nuts—pistachios, pecans, almonds, and peanuts—to your meals. Do not eat large meals a few hours before bed.

A craving is not hunger, and emotional eating leads to weight gain. Self-medicating with food will put you in the six-hundred-pound club—and you do not want that.

Calorie intake matters. The recommended dietary allowance for macronutrients (fats, proteins, carbs, and minerals) can be looked up on the internet. Keep track of what you eat for a few days to get an idea of the amount you eat. Also, there is information online about macros that can help you arrive at your food goals.

Different foods have different profiles and benefits. Do not eat for the sake of eating. The more you think about the nutritional value of what goes into your mouth, the more selective you will become. Fat Secret is one of the best calorie-counting apps. Check it out.

If you can, employ a registered dietician to guide you through the maze of information on dieting and weight loss. A good blend of food groups in small portions will help lower body weight, body fat, and your waistline. Your body needs nutrients to function, but any excess will be stored in your stomach, waist, butt, arms, legs, neck, or face.

Again, you are what you eat. Take care of your body, and your body will take care of you. Do what you can to eat right and stay within your normal weight range.

You can eat anything, but you cannot eat everything. No matter what you eat, eat in moderation. Drink at least eight glasses of water daily—enough to urinate about every three hours. It is important to be familiar with your body mass index (BMI). Your BMI measures your body size in relation to your height and weight. A normal, healthy BMI is in the 18.5–24.9 range. A BMI of twenty-five to thirty is overweight, and a BMI above thirty is obese. The farther out of the normal BMI range you are, the more health risks you have.

It is important to stay at a healthy weight, but how much of your weight is muscle instead of fat is also key. Muscle burns more calories than fat. The biggest reasons for extra pounds are a slower metabolism and less muscle mass. Also, with age, metabolism slows down.

Habits that could wreck your health include binging on alcohol and smoking. Also, snacking all day and consuming more than two thousand calories per day while being a couch potato will do you in. A sedentary lifestyle is not the way to go. Check your vices.

Watch your weight. Maintain a healthy weight. Being underweight is as much of a problem as being overweight. Be within the recommended weight range for your age, height, and body type. Keep a scale in your house and weigh yourself regularly. Do not wait for your weight to be out of control to do something. Seek professional help, including from your school counselors.

Once you are overweight, your health risks increase. You can become a magnet for bad health conditions. Do not blame others if you fall off the diet bandwagon. Take responsibility for what you eat because you are what you eat. Again, calorie intake matters. Portion size matters. Plate content matters.

Balancing nutrition and an active lifestyle is like a high-wire act, but practice makes perfect. Your everyday living matters. Do not be a couch potato. Get up and move around. Get a personal trainer if you need help. The benefits of regular exercise and a healthy diet are priceless.

Physical fitness is a function of good health. Exercise is an effective weight-management tool, and it helps tone your body. There is feel-good effect from exercise. When you do not exercise, you can experience weight gain and loss of muscle mass and strength. Exercise will help you lose fat, gain muscle, and get stronger. To defy muscle atrophy, get moving daily.

About ten thousand daily steps are recommended. If you want to be moderately active, walk about two to three miles daily. You may do a combination of aerobic activities (jogging, stair climbing, etc.) for cardiovascular health and anaerobic exercises for strengthening your muscles and joints.

You may do strength training with weight machines, handheld free weights, resistance bands, or body weight. There are no excuses. It is best to build muscle with progressive overload doing compound exercises: dead lift, bench press, shoulder press, and pull-ups.

Your body is like a machine, and it needs maintenance. Exercise will improve your blood circulation and tune up your body. Your healthy body will work like an open parachute floating in the sky compared to your unhealthy self dropping to the bottom like lead dropped in water.

You may consider these exercise regimen options. Option 1: Five-day training (two days of anaerobic and three days of aerobic or vice versa) with two rest days. Option 2: Four-day training (anaerobic and aerobic as you desire) with three rest days. Your workout goal should be no less than an hour of aerobic or anaerobic training per session. Focus on working on a particular part of your body or your whole body; it is your choice. You are only as strong as your weakest link. Keep your whole body in shape.

Do not neglect pre-workout and post-workout exercises. A few stretches and calisthenics will suffice. Spend about ten minutes at the front end (warm-up stretches) and back end (cool-down stretches). Warming up is more dynamic and improves blood flow. Cooling down is more static, which helps lower your heart rate.

You may experience delayed onset muscle soreness after a workout. Post-workout pain and swelling, after about six hours of activity, is normal. There is no harm in continuing your exercise routine with the soreness if you can. If not, rest your muscles and expect the pain to recede within four days.

To avoid overtraining, give your body and muscles time to recover. You can return to training with more vigor. Two or three rest days is ample recovery time for most people.

Do not overtrain or slack off in the name of recovery. Your excuse for not training will beget more excuses, and you might never run out of excuses.

Motivation is the force behind action. Looking good and feeling good should motivate you. Look at yourself in the mirror every day. Do you like what you see, particularly your side view? Do not buy that men are as old as they feel and women are as old as they look. That is a fallacy. There is no trade-off for an active lifestyle and healthy dieting. Your decision to exercise is in your hands. Blame no one if you do not stick to your plan.

As a younger person, the more you live a health-conscious lifestyle, the better position you will be to manage midlife changes when you get there. Good health is financial stock. Bad health will cost you more than money—and it is one of the sources of poor quality of life. Start early to preserve your health.

At some point, expect to be sick regardless of what you do. Keep up with your periodic medical wellness exams and checkups. That is a good time to share your medical concerns and ask questions of the medical providers. You may get advice like having up to thirty minutes in the sun to obtain your daily dose of vitamin D. Get your vaccinations and seasonal flu shots. If you eat a lot of fast food, you will pack on the pounds. Sleep about eight hours per night for a healthy life. Keep up with your hand-washing hygiene. Learn from the doctors who wash their hands regularly. Do not neglect your dental health. Preventive care is better than curing care.

Every home has a "Doctor Mom" to stock up the medicine cabinets with lots of over-the-counter painkillers and cold, flu, and headache medicines. For whatever reason, these important home medical devices (scale, thermometer, and blood pressure monitor) have not taken their rightful place in every household. All of them should be in your home. Ignoring home medical devices is a risk to healthy living. They help provide early warning signs. The accepted average human temperature is 98.6 degrees Fahrenheit. Normal blood pressure is under 120 (systolic) and 80 (diastolic). Systolic is the pressure during a heartbeat, and diastolic is the pressure between the heartbeats. A scale is essential for determining BMI. Check your vitals periodically. If your readings are consistently off the mark, you may have a problem. Wait no more. Make an appointment to see a medical professional for a closer look at your condition. Undiagnosed and untreated health conditions can lead to death faster. It's better to be safe than dead.

You may be strong now and feel invincible, but change is coming. Look at your parents and older relatives, and you are likely to look like them as you gain more gray hairs. Wrinkles, age spots, and skin blotches will come. If you are lucky enough to live as long as your parents, their look now is an image of your future self. After years, you will be facing your humanity.

To improve your odds, uphold your parents' virtues and replace their vices with more virtues. Death does not care who dies first, but you can do your best to not need the medicine cabinet. An active lifestyle and healthy habits will go a long way in keeping you healthy—and can give you a long life. Watch out for your family history.

Don't worry about your health too much to a fault. Doing so can be a problem. Accept some of the wear and tear of your body.

It is part of the aging process. Manage your physical strength and expectations. As you age, past midlife, your metabolism will slow down. You are more likely to gain extra pounds. Accept the new you while you actively continue to manage your diet and exercise routines. Do not overmedicate for pain. Everybody experiences some pain that come with old age. Your required medical exams should not be skipped. It is very important to identify chronic health problems early and manage them to improve your quality of life. It is not necessarily how long you live; it is your health along the way that counts.

◆ ◆ ◆

Becoming a senior citizen is a rite that comes with long life, wisdom, and crystalized ways of living. Seniors tend to be more candid about life in general and their lives in particular. Pick your parents' brains and learn what you can before their mental, cognitive, and emotional stocks plunge into diminishing returns. You may notice their brains are not as sharp as they used to be or their forgetfulness and increased dependency on others.

Get your parents to talk about their pasts as far back as they can remember. Reminisce and laugh about the good times. Take the time and opportunity to write down their oral history down before they pass. Testimony is good, but evidence is better. The evidence can be inclusive—but not conclusive. The absence of evidence is something. Oral history is secondhand news. Of course, once you know about the past, it becomes your duty to keep it alive. If the crime does not get you, the cover-up will. Parents are more open to telling all when they are closer to eighty.

Expect many health conditions to besiege your parents as they age. Be prepared to support them physically, morally, and otherwise. If you cannot personally be there for them, get them professional assistance.

Many old folks measure events with what they know, which can be overtaken by new parameters. Be understanding, patient, and compassionate with your aging parents. It may not be unimaginable for your aging parents to start acting like children. That is life.

Control your fears. Accept the inevitability of the aging process. When that time comes, assume the reverse role of being a dutiful "child-parent" to them. The student will become the master, and the master will become the student.

No matter what, respect your parents. Secure their buy-in for things that improve their quality of life. Seek their affirmation while helping them. Enable them to live out the lives they desire. Come rain, come shine, never forget your duty to look after your aging parents. We live on borrowed time. Cherish your aging parents and give them attention and tender loving care.

Aging is a fact of life. You cannot stop aging, but you can slow it down and prolong your youthfulness by having a healthy lifestyle and avoiding risky behaviors. The best defense against loss of muscle is strengthening exercises two to three times each week.

At the final call, no one lives forever. Eventually, the infirmities from aging will catch up with you. Old age can slow the gears of the mind. Joint issues (knees, shoulders, hips, and spines), cognitive, vision, hearing, dementia, organ failure, and more ailments will start setting off the expiration alert warnings.

For a healthy tomorrow, start living healthy now. Good health, other than predisposed conditions, is part of a well-led life.

CHAPTER 9

LEADERSHIP

GG says leadership is serious business. It is like the oxygen you breathe. It is critical and nearly invisible. When it is lacking, chaos and panic reign. When leadership is good, things go swimmingly, and people are generally nonchalant about it. Fortunately, you are uniquely gifted to manage and lead yourself. You must lead yourself before leading anyone else. Your actions and inactions will determine if you are a good or bad leader.

Leadership is partly an art and partly a science, and it requires some finesse to reach the summit. Leadership is a developed experience. You learn from those who came before you. Your exposure to various leadership qualities will help with molding your own leadership style. When you are on top of the leadership ladder, you will be on your own. You will be the source of light and achieve your desired results.

The appropriate time to learn and grow is when you are moving up the leadership ladder. As an average person coming up the leadership ladder, there is a lot to know and do. You probably learned most of the things you know as a leader in your budding years. Therefore, it is important to appreciate any job you have, small or big, see it as an opportunity to get to your dream leadership style.

It takes work to become a successful leader. As a junior, you will learn from the seniors. You will be a senior someday. It does not happen overnight. Now is the time to build the essential experiences you can draw from in emergency when you do not have the luxury of time to plan how to lead. You can devote one hour a day, six days each week, to being the kind of leader you want to be. Take the time to discover what good and successful leadership is. Learn it, practice it, and hone your skills.

Make continuous learning part of your daily objectives because that knowledge will help curb your fatal optimism and shave down any cynical tendencies. It will help you see the operational landscape and plan ahead. Of course, you cannot plan for everything. Leave room on your schedule to allow flexibility for dealing with emergencies. Never clutter your calendar.

No matter the situation, do not let should have, would have, or could have deflate your senses. Fair is fair, right is right, and wrong is wrong. Always act with honor and dignity.

The leadership skills you acquire will help you move up in the ranks. With time and experience, you will get to supervise others. Emerging leaders tend to compete against the standards and not against their coworkers. They support whoever the leaders are and make them look good. They do not bad-mouth others behind their backs. They are team players. They are reliable, carry their own crosses, and seek guidance when they are in doubt. They accept responsibility for their own actions and inactions. They are straight shooters. They do not sugarcoat the truth. They offer timely recommendations and support their leaders' decisions.

Self-starters, can-do attitude, positive energy, and team spirit are attributes of good leaders. They understand nothing is perfect, and they do their best every day to improve their businesses. Overall, they are good at what they do, and they can fill in for their superiors. They are ready to move up when the "next man up" call comes.

Leaders need to make decisions. You make decisions every day. Some of your personal and work-life decisions profoundly impact others. Your action or inaction matters. Right or wrong, make a decision. It is better than freezing up. Decide to make a difference. Then act. Make course corrections as required.

If your superior thinks something is important, it is important. Determine what is asked for versus what is wanted. Do the "asked for" part first. Always ask your supervisor how you can support the team. If your peers or subordinates attach importance to something, respect it. Figure out how to oblige.

Team up and learn fast. Learn everything you can from everybody you can, and you will never stop improving. Understand the lay of the land. Learn what is not on the organizational chart: palace intrigue, team chemistry, and matrix relationships. Help your team identify the weak links and focus on relieving any pain. Consider upstream and downstream impacts. Show the team that what matters to them matters to you.

Act like you understand you are not indispensable. The organization is bigger than you. Refuse to be arrogant. Be authentic and humble. Do not fake it. People can smell bullshit a mile away. It is not what you know that is important; it is what you do with it that earns you respect.

Leaders have to zoom out and zoom in. They have to decide what to leave in and leave out. Watch what you say, when you say it, and how you say it. Communicate—and then have the physical and moral courage to do what you say.

Many situations are relative and contextual, and deciding what not to do is important. You always have three options: freeze, fight, or flight. The way you respond matters. Listen to the music and dance to the tune; otherwise, you will be dancing offbeat and drawing unwanted attention.

Excellence is not a fluke. It comes from the mosaic of your cultivated habits. You are what you repeatedly do. Stay vigilant. Anticipate problems. Do not blame others. Accept responsibility. Prepare to work in a multigenerational workforce, play in office politics, and win. A strong desire to positively affect others' lives is a mark of good leaders.

It is a strength to acknowledge what you do not know. It will ease the pressure on you and show others that you are open to receiving help. Some people give help, and some receive help. That is life. Seek help when you need it.

Delegate your weaknesses to others who may use the opportunity to showcase their strengths. Capitalize on others' strengths and rely on them to minimize your weaknesses. Leadership is getting the right things done through other people.

As you face your arduous leadership challenges, actively seek and learn the correct combinations to open the golden door. Patience is a virtue, and you must hold it close to the heart. Be positive, but don't expect easy days.

Hold your values and high esteem and never sell them. If you find yourself transgressing, you have lost your moral and spiritual moorings. Under pressure, you may cave to the path of least resistance rather than doing the right thing. That is selfish. Never lack courage.

To help you get the cattle into the barn, have a rebirth in your belief in God. With faith in God, like Daniel, you can be thrown into the lions' den and come out without a scratch.

Be human and vulnerable like a normal person. Act like you pass gas and have bowel movements like everybody else—one to three times daily with successive stool texture going from solid to soft, softer to pencil-like, and then watery. What happens when you turn off the light? We are all the same. We are all shadows. Show humility, emotions, and empathy.

Good leaders maintain a culture of honesty and transparency. Delayed obedience is disobedience. Bring common sense to bear and do not leave it at the door. Publicly praise, but rebuke with grace in private. Know the limelight can be blinding on the stage, and the applause ends with your exit from the stage.

Know team members' areas of natural excellence. If anyone is struggling, ask how you can be of help. Genuinely lend a helping hand. You can write the check and let someone else do the heavy lifting. The key is to show a great desire to help others and act on it. Beam with enthusiasm when you congratulate other people and show empathy when you console them.

When you treat people like people, they become people—not equipment without feelings. When you recognize people where they are, they will not forget how you make them feel. In turn, they will reciprocate. People respect those they admire.

Your relationships affect everything you do. With good relationships, people will go out of their way to do you a favor. A bad relationship is a recipe for disaster. It is a curse. It brings disunity, which can make the simplest tasks difficult and as dangerous as climbing K2.

Your reputation is everything. It will precede you. A bad reputation stinks like a skunk from many feet away. A good reputation is adoring and priceless.

Be shrewd. There will be plenty of situations to test and validate your optimism. Get them right. Many people like positive energy. Embrace it. Do not be a prophet of doom. Cynicism is a cancer. Instead, live and project a positive attitude. Dwell more on positive things instead of following the more natural path to criticize, condemn, and complain. Object to people who often criticize others. Object to people who get their high from belittling others. Be the sunshine person, and your attitude will be contagious.

Learn to be a team player and carry your own load and some more. No one wants a deadwood team member. Read the team's playbook. Study it. Act on it. Measure it. Review it. Reorient it and continue to improve it. Success will beget more success. Appreciate being part of the team. See the team as a special bunch who believes to whom much is given, much is expected. Frame your successes in terms of the impact you make on the overall goal. Be the team member who knows that cover six is more than standing at the back. Push beyond your comfort zone for the good of the team. Be among the first to take blame and the last to take credit. Hold yourself to higher standards; that is contagious.

Be the star of the team. You cannot rest on your laurels. If you hang on your glory days, your relevance will fade like an evening shadow. Be prepared to say what need to be said and do what needs to be done. Then seek 360-degree feedback.

Show passion and zeal. Exhibit knowledge. Handle trust in a manner that makes others trust you more. Inspire respect. Learn that every problem has a soft spot. Watch a lion attacking another animal's neck or wild dogs attacking another animal's rear end. Look for weak links. Giants are big and strong, but they are slow. No wonder David took down Goliath. If you raise a problem, come up with the recommendations to solve it.

To draw the right attention and resources, prioritize issues into two buckets: above-line buckets and below-line buckets. Break down the list into short-term and long-term solutions. Everything should not be critical.

During meetings and conversations, listen more and talk less. If you listen to people as much as you hear them, you will not miss out in life. Look for current and relevant firsthand perspectives and research work results. On hot-button issues, it is best to hear the proposition's case and the opposing viewpoints, before voicing your position. When you make thoughtful comments or questions at the right times, you will command respect as someone who is levelheaded. Speak up only when you have heard enough on both sides of the issue. As a leader, if you speak too early, you may send the wrong signal and skew the entire deliberation.

Search for the virtues in others; everybody is good at something. There's something interesting in everyone. Recognize it; for the beneficiary, a small win is still a win.

Do not consider yourself superior to others. Consider others as your coworkers or teammates. Your juniors are never your servants, and you should never treat others as your servants.

Do not be critical of a person; instead, be critical of the conduct. The big door of leadership swings on a small hinge of character. Stellar character is priceless.

Practice what you preach. Your actions must speak louder than your words. Leadership is more about actions than words.

Avoid double standards and hypocrisy. Do the right things when no one is looking. Avoid unethical and illegal acts like the plague. Know that clean character is a boon to earning the trust of well-meaning people.

There are backstories and front stories in every situation. There are no less than two sides to any story—positive and negative—and each tells a human story. Look inside to understand the why of what happened. Know when to provide the exact type of leadership the team members need: directive, participatory, or delegative leadership.

Prepare to be either a peace maker or peacekeeper—and accept the costs of either choice. The problem child will suck up more energy and time. With your Midas touch, inspire the feuding parties to live peacefully.

Learn to embrace and establish systems that amplify people's strengths and improve their weaknesses. Preach and maintain high standards. What you ignore, you empower. State it loud and clear—no one is above the law or untouchable.

Compel others to actions to get results and sacrifice for the greater good. Your reputation for creating a winning culture wherever you lead will put you in demand and in play for future assignments.

Be proactive in nature and learn to see the big picture. Think macro first and then get micro. See things in mosaic form. Dissect them into clean blocks for the layperson to comprehend. Plan ahead and adjust your fire as the targets move.

There is strength in numbers, and two heads are better than one. Seek and get subordinates' input. Secure their buy-in for any actions that need to be taken.

Leadership is an everyday event. Plant the seed in good soil. Water it. Weed it. Prune it. Labor to harvest the yield and discard the chaff. The trees you plant may not benefit you directly, but they will provide shade for generations after you.

Life is not a fine line, and some things beyond your control will happen. Burning the boat you arrived in will make retreat impossible. Uneasy is the head that wears the crown. Develop mental toughness that holds well under pressure, and a calm temperament will minimize unforced errors. Once you notice an unforced error, correct it.

Leadership development is a deliberate process, and good leadership does not magically happen. A lot of learning occurs to refine natural abilities. It takes a lot of practice to become comfortable at the helm.

As you mature, manage by objective. Trust your subordinates to cover the rest of the enterprise. Make your subordinates feel important as you put the carrot-and-stick theory in motion. Watch out for the point of diminishing returns and make on-time corrections. Delegation is not fire and forget. You can delegate responsibilities, but the accountability still rests with you.

With your power, you can do bad things that could make stones cry. Evil cannot be wholesomely undone. When it is cut and retied, the length is never the same.

You sit on the fulcrum of balance of power. In your decisions and actions, always think of the impact you have on others. Be authentic, humble, visible, and reachable. Know when to change and play different roles: decision maker, observer, teacher, consultant, mentor, or sounding board. Your reputation is everything, and your character is your reputation. Aspire not to lose your currency; if you do, you will be no good to the people you lead. Try not to compromise your honor and integrity. Your values should not be purchased for any price. Banish corruption. Do what is right when no one is looking.

Place high value on people's ideas and talents. Recognize stars in the organization, keep people with potentials on your radar, and cultivate leaders. Constantly upgrade your skill sets. Avoid paralysis by analysis. Avoid using intimidation or fear to motivate others. Don't be a prima donna. You are a leader to serve the led. You should be the strongest advocate for your people. Be fair to all.

Integrate equal-opportunity programs in your organization. Be a person who works well with the top, middle, and bottom echelons. Break down silos that divide people. Build functional, beautiful bridges.

Display an attitude that shows you work with me not for me. This attitude will put your humility on display. Your respect for the dignity of your coworkers as important partners in the workforce will nurture pride and breed a sense of ownership. Show them you care about their goals, dreams, and desires. Invest in the success of others by putting a support system in place. Inspire them to greatness. At the end of the day, leave others better than you found them.

Good leaders are hungry to learn. Read, stay current and relevant, and encourage others to do the same. Teach what right looks like. Coach, counsel, and mentor your subordinates. Encourage professional growth and create a deep bench for your organization.

With a "we and us mentality," you can gain followers' trust and loyalty.

As the Bible says, by their actions you shall know them. Subordinates can see through the smoke. The leaders who care about them earn their trust. Those subordinates will go to hell and back for those leaders. They will produce and meet or exceed targets.

Ask open-ended questions and patiently listen to the full responses. Those in power can miss the point, and folks not in power can come up with great ideas. Learn from the weakest members in the team as much as from the strongest.

Fresh wind clears the cobwebs of complacency. Always be on the lookout for new ideas to get rid of bottlenecks. Stay nimble and work smart. Improve conditions and make an impact. You will build a capacity for transitional knowledge, and the older workers can learn from younger ones who are savvy in new technology and contemporary affairs. When appropriate, give up the old ways and embrace the new ways. Find ways to belong and not be left behind. Show them that leadership is doing the right things while management is doing things right.

Everybody has the power to make others happy. Some people make others happy by entering the room, and others make people happy by leaving the room. Which group are you? How you make others feel about themselves says a lot about you.

Surround yourself with the right people—great minds—when discussing serious matters and real ideas. When the discussion is about events, average minds can take the seats. Small-minded people can come in and play when needed. Surprise. Results come from knowing how to bring out the best in people.

As a leader, know when to proceed with caution. Your speed dictates the speed of the team. You are responsible for the health of the team. You are remembered by the doors you open or close for others.

Know the importance of time. You bring out the best in people, and you make their drop of rain on a leaf shine like a pearl. Without you helping them find themselves, the same raindrop will fall into the ocean and be lost forever. Help subordinates recognize the components under the hood of the car. Show them what makes the car run. Teach them that each person will work with others at different times, and everyone has a personal stake for the team to succeed. Help them align their thinking with reality, put things in perspective, and not get lost in their emotions. Ultimately, help everyone win at something.

When you think you have done enough, do some more before, during, and after the objective. Good leaders know ways to stretch talents until holes appear and then enable the mending of the holes.

Good leaders bring out the angels in people, help them recognize the picture making them happy, and reinforce their belief in self, country, and God. Good leaders empower you to know your worth and set your own price. If you ask for less, you get less. If you ask for more, you get more.

Because the led are a reflection of their leaders, if they are jacked up, their leaders are jacked up too. Good leaders lead by example. They are approachable and empathetic, and they make people feel their positive energy and presence. They show remarkable impulse control. They do not forget their charges need recognition and validation. They routinely reward maximum efforts and positive results. They set up systems. There is a place for everything, and everything is in its place. Because they practice right, they don't do things wrong.

Good leaders run like a thermostat, quietly in the background without requiring attention until something breaks, and then everybody notices.

On Top of the Ladder

When you are on top of the ladder, you have a choice to be a good leader or a bad leader. Take your pick. Good leaders focus on people, and they are good at solving problems. They have the wisdom to know the right things and the courage to do things right. *They focus on people.* One of the major things you should do is be a people-focused leader. You win with people. Work on the premise that everybody is beautiful, depending on what you are looking for. Each individual is different in capacity, interests, goals, and talents. Look for the tree in the forest. Look for unvarnished diamonds—people with talent—and turn them into polished diamonds.

Find the needle in the haystack. Grow and harvest talent for today and tomorrow. Build a deep bench of talent. Nurture and develop followers to be leaders. Enable people to develop to their fullest potential in the roles they can fill best.

When a person misbehaves—not grossly—address the misconduct, and do not attack the person. Make an effort to help the person improve rather than getting rid of the person and hiring and training a replacement.

Take care of people, and the people will take care of you, things, and the organization.

Leadership is reaction between you, your followers, and the situation. Be astute in leveraging the power of downward dependence. Success hinges on people—the janitors, receptionists, supervisors, and directors—across your organization.

See what is good about a person as dog lovers do in cherishing their dogs' instincts for companionship, protection, or hunting.

People follow leaders who stand up for them. Cover your people and assure them that nothing will stand in the way of excellence. Give them your word that we are all in this together. The more you care, the more you can protect.

Speak with humility. Speak to persuade, inform, and invite. Respect your audience. Supervise as you would like to be supervised. Great leaders are great servants. Nothing speaks to it like leaders eating last—metaphorically and in reality. Being fair is among the best traits of good leaders. Inspiring and uplifting others is another. Impress upon your people that their destiny is not failure; it is greatness. Give people hope. Give people a voice.

Respect team members' seniority and order of merit when developing subordinate leaders into a high-performing team. Have subordinate leaders sit in periodically on leadership roles to show them what the higher responsibilities entail.

To eliminate pecking order turbulence—as seen in the disruption of buffalos or geese in flight—establish order of succession in the organization. Doing so allows subordinates to manage their expectations and be ready for new dynamics as the team formation changes.

Know your impact on people. Get results through people while building the next generation. Inspire people to challenge the status quo and do things that appear impossible at first glance.

Encourage people to have original initiatives and pride and ownership of solutions. When your subordinates believe in you, they will rise to the occasion. Because they know you have faith in them and consider them valued members of the team, they will do their best to live up to your expectations.

Genuinely care about subordinates' well-being at work and at home. Show empathy and talk to people like they matter. Do not let your mouth disengage from your brain. Hurtful words can pierce the soul more than physical lashes on the body.

Sometimes, what counts is not what you said, but the context in which it was said. Be approachable and down-to-earth. Care enough to get to know your subordinates' personal details by gaining their trust to confide in you as someone who can help improve their situation. Loose lips sink ships. Good leaders keep subordinates' privileged information airtight. Leadership flourishes where good relationship exit. Good leaders draw people out. There is no shortcut to building healthy relationships. Help protégés realize their dreams. Routinely do the right things to stay in people's good graces. Enable people to reach and maintain excellence. Surviving the Serengeti requires doing your best for others while they are doing their best for you. No person is independent. You live in an interdependent world. Your survival and success pretty much come from how well you strike a balance in what others give or take from you and vice versa.

We are all works in progress, but you should be making concerted effort to invest in followers and develop them into leaders-in-waiting. Put in the systems and processes to look the part and truly open doors for budding leaders.

From observation and practice, protégés must learn the finesse of the orchestra conductor turning his back to the crowd or a rap singer facing the crowd. How you lead depends on the situation.

Good leaders strive for diversity and inclusiveness in their workforce because people come to the table with unique cultures and experiences. When you weave individual strings together, you can bind an elephant that could not be restrained with a single string. With everyone's best effort, it is easier to achieve team excellence.

Solve problems. As a good leader, when solving problems, embrace some form of these six elements. The order is not necessarily sequential; it can run concurrent as the case may be. Let the situation drive the agenda.

First, excel at bringing people, subject matter experts included, together. Leverage the power of their diversity to redefine the problems and find short-term and long-term solutions.

Second, when you give an order, link what must be done to why it needs to be done. Allowing subordinates to recommend how best things can be done is a common practice of good leaders. After you introduce the situation, sit back, treat everyone as a partner, and listen to as many people as the circumstance permits. Is the plan supportable with the resources on hand? If yes, ask for the culmination point. When the plan is not supportable, address the shortfalls or adjust and refine the plan.

With eagle eyes, during the discussions, pick up on the points and address any blind spots. Beside your initial and intervening guidance, speak last to put meat on the bones. Summarize takeaways and reaffirm the acceptable risks and your decision.

In tandem, conduct risk analysis and determine mitigations. Determine your critical organizational metrics and make them inspectable items. Periodic inspection shows which areas are important to you.

Third, conduct follow-ups. Start with the confirmation briefing. Soon after getting tasked, subordinates should repeat their understanding of the assigned tasks. It will help to clear up any confusion and misunderstanding from the get-go.

Ensure that teams know their expectations. Ensure that the goals and strategies are clear. Have theme and nested programs. Determine priorities with milestones and accompanying deliverables. Someone or some office must be assigned to each of the activities. The deliverable products should include established systems, standards, processes, and metrics as the mission dictates.

Next, conduct in-progress reviews (IPR). This crucial step monitors progress and keeps work on schedule. The frequency of IPR will be situation dependent. Program capstone out-brief and after-action-review at the tail end. The after-action report will highlight lessons learned and the way ahead.

Fourth, put the systems in place and get the systems and people to work together like clockwork. It is easy to break a single broom, but it is nearly impossible to break bundled brooms. Talk results and impacts.

Fifth, do not lead by just sitting behind the executive desk in your corner office. Visit frontline workers frequently, but do not pester them. There is nothing like witnessing events yourself, and feeling the conditions will definitely improve your perspectives. On your visits, express appreciation for subordinates' contributions. Give them updates on the organization's outlook. They will welcome news about the health of their organization and recognition for their contributions.

Ensure current and relevant information is available to those who need to know. Information is power you share with the led. Done right, it empowers people. When information is deficient, the rumor mill takes over the communication bloodstream. Also, poor information creates a void, breeding distrust.

Sixth, be fair and firm across the board. Underwrite honest mistakes. Delegate responsibility. Retain accountability. Inspire and empower all—and then fade into the background like the air we breathe.

Ensure periodic individual performance counseling is one of your people-development metrics. People appreciate constructive feedback on what they are doing well and need to sustain and areas of improvement with pointers for how to do better.

On a reoccurring basis, recognize high-performing people by publicly saying thank you for a job well done or giving awards or promotions. Everyone wants to be appreciated, and no one wants to remain at the bottom. Know the power of incentive and tap it to the fullest to build and keep team pride high.

Part of your job as the leader is to build a culture that unleashes and harnesses subordinates' initiatives and gains their buy-in on the work at hand. Be open to protest and welcome protest. For courage, think about David taking on Goliath and defeating him. For wisdom, Solomon identified the true birth mother by offering to cut up the baby. The imposter mother agreed to have the baby divided, but the birth mother wanted the baby whole and alive.

For taking bad counsel, Rehoboam listened to his peers, and they stroked his ego. Judas betrayed Christ. Rich lessons are all over the Bible, and they are available to learn from and to help you build your team.

Whoever is in charge should be in charge. Support whoever the leaders are. They should be comfortable in their own skin and command the confidence of superiors, peers, and subordinates. They should give credit to whomever credit is due. Chastise in private, but praise in public. Celebrate successes and often say thank you for a job well done. Genuinely smile along when the joke is on you. A bad leader will only smile, ear to ear, when the joke is at someone else's expense.

Your actions as a good leader will foster unit pride and high esprit de corps. You will have happier teams and positive results. Your impacts and importance will come to the surface soon after being replaced by a bad leader. If you do not want to be a bad leader, good. A glimpse of what bad leaders look like will help you reaffirm that choice. They are self-centered, treat others awful, and have decision issues.

They are self-centered. Bad leaders often have a superiority complex, and they act like demigods. They think they know it all and have a monopoly on knowledge and wisdom. They feel indispensable and are self-deceiving. No matter how good or bad a dancer is, they must leave the stage at some point.

Bad leaders forget they are not the best; they were just given the privilege to serve the people. Unfortunately, bad leaders are the last to realize they are not good at the jobs they were hired to do.

Bad leaders often toot their own horns. They wallow in self-pontification in front of a captive audience. They enjoy listening to the sound of their own voices while glowing in self-glorification. They want everything about the organization to revolve around them. They lose balance from the huge chip on their shoulders. They want to be worshipped like a dictator or a deity. *They treat others awfully.* Bad leaders have disdain for messengers with bad news. When information is unfiltered, they go berserk. Even good news may not be good enough. They have to be padded to make them rosier. Bad leaders tend to have a hard time dealing with negative feedback, and they are likely to skin the messenger.

Being quick to anger is common among bad leaders. In rage, they throw out the baby with the bathwater. The solution to a headache is not cutting off the head. Bad leaders tend to pervade the organizational culture with a vindictive, take-no-prisoners approach. They lack empathy, particularly for those not in their close circle of friends. The ones they see as outcasts are rarely groomed for progression. They deny the outcasts a prong on the ladder to the next level.

For little or no reason, they go on tirades and belittle others publicly to stroke their egos. They are disrespectful and lord over their subordinates. They are likely to be reactive and overreactive.

They usually spare their own skins while providing no cover for their subordinates' honest mistakes. When things turn out well, they take the credit. When things go wrong, they are quick to throw subordinates under the bus.

Bad leaders see anyone with different viewpoints as an enemy and sideline the person. Bad leaders will criticize more than they will compliment. They are standoffish. They are afraid of mingling and joking with subordinates unless they are among the handful of yes-men agreeing with them.

Bad leaders have decision issues. Bad leaders throw fairness out the window and dish out preferential treatment at the mercy of their whims and caprices. They allow their biases to cloud their decisions. Bad leaders wait until the cows come home to make decision. A decision delayed is justice denied.

They are prone to making bad decisions, which wastes resources. Their unsound decisions send others on wild goose chases—wasting people's time—and they put subordinates in harm's way.

They lead by fear and intimidation. Otherwise, no one will keep their verbalized and published standards. Their standards are not worth the paper they are printed on. Their words ring hollow—do like they say, but not like they do.

Bad leaders are known for being micromanagers, which stifles subordinates' initiatives. They withhold information to make themselves seem important as the only ones who know. They demand that tasks must be done, and they do not care how you get them done or the collateral damage.

Leading by example is not their hallmark. They talk the talk, but they go missing in action when it is time to walk the talk. Bad leaders are wrecking balls. They bring a toxic work environment and poor productivity. Many employees hate working with or for them. As soon as bad leaders are unprotected by the status bubble, their employees spill their guts about the misery of working for them. Bad leaders are like having a toothache.

Are you a good leader or a bad leader? It's your choice.

CHAPTER 10

PUBLIC SPEAKING

GG says public speaking skills will set you apart in the big leagues. The benefit of being a good speaker is immeasurable. People will look up to you to speak up for them. You will stand head and shoulders above the masses. Being good at public speaking is a gateway to leadership opportunities.

Many things come naturally to many people—but not public speaking. Some form of nervous energy comes with the territory. Those who are good at it tend to have better handle on their nervousness. They get the butterflies in their stomachs to fly in formation.

The way to be a good public speaker is to study the craft and practice it. It's best to have your eyes on orators of your liking. Try to mirror the examples that complement your character.

Wordplay and sentence sequencing are valueless. Delivery is as important as substance. Excellent public speakers share facts in story form, and some use humor to get and keep the audience's attention. Few people are natural-born speakers' public speaking is more or less an acquired skill. If you want to be a good one, start building your vocabulary early in life. Learn three to five new words or figures of speech a week—and try to incorporate the words into your daily conversations.

Along with building your word power, practice wordplay for special effects. Orators master figures of speech. They string common words into new forms and memorable, strong expressions. You can be the orator among your peers or your generation.

Your voice is an asset unique to you. Great public speakers have signature voices like no other, which rise and fall like an orchestra to emphasize notes. You hear their voice once, and it registers—and you are willing to listen to more of what they have to say. They sound like they are happy to see their audience. They are good at using figures of speech, stories, antidotes, and humor to move audiences from laughter to tears or the other way around.

They know ideas matter, but kind words go a long way. They know what they say is important—but how they say it is more important. They know the less they speak, the more people hear. The more they talk, the less people remember.

Because words can start a fire, they read the room, know their audience, and tailor their delivery. They are collegial and colloquial. They do not want to become the story and take away from the issue at hand. They mind their p's and q's, use rhetoric and elocution, and make every sentence relevant.

Your rich word power will be on display during public speaking. You have to read voraciously and listen to speeches to know what good ones look like. Persuasively stringing the words in your brain's dictionary is an art honed by serious practice. Great speeches are crafted to leave an imprint on the audience's memory.

Most speakers are nervous, but they overcame it once they start engaging their audiences. Stage fright is universal, but it is manageable when you speak about issues you are prepared to talk about. I have never heard of a public speaker who was not a bit nervous before an important speech. Do not permit nervousness to deter you from public speaking. For better performance, research your topic extensively, prepare, and rehearse the speech delivery.

Research your topic by gathering facts from relevant materials and people. Firsthand perspectives work best. Otherwise, use experts' opinions. Be imaginative. Make the information fresh by adding value and implications for the audience.

A good speech has plenty of white pace and bigger fonts for easy reading with a quick glance. Link relevant historical perspectives to the current perspectives. Have the perfect opening act. Make two to five main points; three points is the sweet spot. Add a perfect closing act.

Keep your speech succinct. Five to eighteen minutes is OK. Twelve minutes is the sweet spot. Keynote speeches are much longer. I prefer ones delivered within twenty-five minutes. When possible, use an appropriate example, short story, humor, or an analogy to make each point. Ensure the points answer the questions that people in the audience want addressed.

Stories are memorable. It is important to have a good transition between points. The story must be nested and flow seamlessly. Flow is the key word. People remember them more.

It is important to deliver your speech within a normal audience's attention. Keep the audience engaged by telling them what you will tell them, then tell them, and summarize the takeaway of what you just told them. At the end of your speech, the audience should walk away with satisfaction. They should feel that listening to you was worthwhile and not a waste of time.

Show your signature style with your words and their arrangement. It is not only what you say; it is how you say it that matters. Before your speech, when you are reading or listening to any communication medium, set your mind's antenna and identify speech artistry. Try to appreciate the unique wordplay or word arrangements. Seek out many good speeches. Dissect them and learn the elements you admire.

Do orators like Winston Churchill, former prime minister of United Kingdom, John Fitzgerald Kennedy, thirty-fifty president of the United States, and Martin Luther king Jr., American Baptist minister and civil rights activist, ring a bell? Have you listened to addresses by William Harry McRaven, retired United States Navy four-star admiral? Have you listened to speeches, particularly "Making Africa Work for Africa" by Patrick Loch Otiena Lumumba, renowned Kenyan professor of public law? These orators' speeches are accessible on YouTube. There is so much to learn from them. They have visionary and audacious messages, unquestionable content, and substance clarity. What was, what is, and what can be? How can we get there? Situation diagnosis and prognosis with possible outcomes laid bare. Past, present, and future interpreted.

Orators should come off as very widely read, informed, and historically equipped. Their gifted signature voices and eloquence should serenade listeners. Their voice modulation helps messages barrel down auditory nerve of mortals. They get and keep your attention. They hold you captive—in a good way. Their powerful ways with words are showcased. They string words into sentences and statements into memorable short stories. Examples and dry humor are highlighted and tied to the main theme. They repeat the themes over and over during their speeches. They conclude with change from what to what.

Other great speakers speak on matters where they have expertise and passion. They put a personal touch and a human face on what would have otherwise sounded like list of academic theories and principles. They tell snappy stories crowned with a theme or repeat the theme to tell stories. Their stories are focused on themes and reoccurring ideas. Each story narrates what was or is, how and why, in support of the theme. One story or one message is tied to the theme. Multiple stories are tied to theme. Great speakers come through with an air of authority and authentic freshness that appeases the audience.

Choose the orators or public speakers you admire most. Flavor their speech style with your personality and make it your signature style. If you put in the hard work, your speech will showcase your efforts for others to admire.

Read aloud when practicing. If a mirror is available, practice in front of it to see yourself as the audience would. Edit your draft speech if something did not flow right or sound right. Accept suggestions if someone is available to provide feedback. By the end of your rehearsal, you should feel confident and feel like an expert. Remember the audience thinks you have the knowledge they need.

To find eloquence in speech delivery, search the speeches by President Ronald Reagan—the Great Communicator, and Congresswoman Barbara Jordan—acclaimed by many as sounding like God. Their voices were special and alluring.

If you are reading the speech, take your eyes off the script, look up to the audience at the end of reading one or two sentences, and look at the sides of the room. At other times, look at the center of the room.

When reading, do not dwell on minor omissions or imperfections; the audience is forgiving. They tend to remember good stories laced with facts and stressed main points.

Some speakers talk fluidly with just their talking points. Make whatever delivery style you are comfortable with your own.

CHAPTER 11

POLITICS

According to GG, whether you are into politics or not, your local and world politics are into you. Politics is people, and politics is government. Your government, good or bad, will depend on the politicians the people support or tolerate. As an electorate, it behooves you to show some interest in the political climate of your time. At the minimum, vote during local and national elections.

Encourage your family and friends to exercise their right to vote. If you are out there in numbers, politicians will respect and court your voting bloc. Do not be the silent majority. Show up and show out like a vocal minority. Voters pick their politicians—and not the other way around.

Politics is like a lottery; you must play to win. You cannot win a lottery you do not play. If you plan to be a politician, you must immerse yourself in the act. There is no trade-off for political shrewdness and savviness. Quick tongue and wit are definite assets. Meritocracy is not an absolute for advancement.

Politics is a duel where the luck factor is negligible. Opponents jump into the lion's den and go for each other's jugulars. Do not expect a savior. There is rarely one. Do not count on politicians' sense of decency. It often falls by the wayside.

Politicians are skilled at diversion, omission, and skirting the obvious. They are very good at redefining facts. Most politician think like lawyers and suggest the handwriting on the wall may be a forgery. They may accept death and taxes as inevitable, but with a caveat—tax burden or lack of it depends on individual income and state of residency. Politicians are known to throw spaghetti on the wall to see if it will stick. Most politicians are very shrewd.

On average, political correctness sells more than the truth. Politicians tend to put their finger in the air, sense the wind direction, and sway in the direction of the audience. They will follow their natural default habit and make the courted voters feel like they are in the same boat.

Politicians live and die by their messaging. Good politicians can easily sell a dead turtle as alive and at rest, retracted in its shell. Buyer beware.

Politicians often profess to be the problem-solvers. Typically, the opposing party gins up policy lever pulls as a remedy to the incumbents' failures and explain how they will turn the bleak picture into rosy garden.

Politicians pick their sides, dig deep chasms, and fuel the feelings of abject despair or utopia among voters. Yes, identity politics sells. They divide and conquer voters by religion, race, or ethnicity—and in unimaginable ways. With crafted displays, politicians build trust based on social intercourse, and they eventually convince voters that they are the anointed one. Politicians take pride in galvanizing followers. Their tactics may be distasteful, but they are not immoral or illegal.

Incumbents and opponents often end up attacking each other's records—distorting them—and their personalities to the chagrin of many voters. No wonder so many people consider politics a dirty game. Most politicians see politics as a means to an end.

Politics should be the art of governance and not dominance. Unfortunately, many people experience it differently. Most politicians toe the party line in governance. The opposing party's agenda rarely sees the daylight. If you talk the state of politics, some people will argue with you like you ate their lunch. Generally, democratic politics come in two dominant narratives: liberal and conservative or left wing and right wing.

Conservatives tend to display tenacious personalities like bulldogs. Liberals have more tolerant personalities like golden retrievers. Conservatives tend to show up for fight with chain saws, and liberals come with butter knives.

Members of both parties have extreme views. The elements are comparably small, but they are loud and exert disproportionate influence. Call them ultra-left and ultra-right wings. Elected representatives are all equal in many respects, but these ultra folks tend to have a large media presence and make themselves look more powerful than they may actually be.

The real world does not lend itself to utopian liberal or conservative ideologies. Arguments in favor of either pure liberalism or conservatism will fall flat on their face.

It is muddled up or even hypocritical when you critically look into individual liberty versus government involvement in people's lives: the government's role in social justice and inequalities, religion and government symbiosis or separation, economic drivers—capitalism or mixed economies—climate change activism or denial, globalization, immigration, and national defense. The ideology platforms can go on and twist your mind. In life and politics, no one size fits all.

Moderates come to the rescue. People with moderate views, swing voters, and independents are inconspicuous until elections or when critical bipartisan bills are desired. That is the lay of the political land.

A lot of people pick and choose their political alignment out of convenience—the one who benefits them most. Some people stick with an ideology due to their family's historical party loyalty and are reluctant to break with tradition. Sometimes, community or even zip code peer pressure is a factor in political affiliation. If one is willing to be honest, a mixed political ideology should be a balance. Be proud to be a moderate if you are one. Center-left or center-right-leaning moderates tend to build a united front for the common good.

We are not political animals by accident. No one lives on an island, self-sufficient and sustainable with everything life has to offer. We are part of the ecosystem. Whether we accept it or not, to some degree, we must depend on others to survive, succeed, thrive, and live our best lives.

When two or more are gathered, it does not take long for a pecking order to emerge—leaders and followers and group or party allegiance. Can you imagine a ship without a captain or a pot of soup salted by multiple cooks? Disaster. No wonder, any given community with hundreds, thousands, or millions of people goes through the agony of adopting a political system to suit their perceived interests.

Politics may be a dirty game, but it is a necessity. It is a means to an end. Somebody has to govern the community and country, right? Democratic politics may have challenges, but its offerings of equal representation, transparent individual liberty, and transparent accountable governance—when done well—can be liberating for all and worth the hassle.

You can choose to be a spectator on the sideline or actively participate in the political grinder and the rough-and-tumble diplomacy. As a citizen in good standing, do not exclude yourself from the process. Embrace it, exercise your voting franchise, and find your place in your political life. You can even run for political office and make a mark.

A lot of young, aspiring politicians yearn to serve their communities. They tend to volunteer their time and have some ideals. They seek opportunities to show up and participate for a given cause. They tend to be at the forefront of public discourse to magnify and amplify issues of their interests and passions. They get into the good trouble and demonstrate a willingness to sacrifice for a cause bigger than themselves.

Political aspirants try to convince people that they are one of them. They are cut from the same thread, and they feel the pain as much as anyone in the community: They profess to be smart about their local situations and want solutions to problems. They carry themselves as capable of reaching across the aisle to reach a consensus. They have some degree of charisma and pull people to them. They smile easily and come across as friendly. A good number of them are eloquent. They win the hearts and minds of the people. They are pretty good at building rapport and earning trust. Most would-be politicians have no problems with public speaking. They meet voters at wherever venues there are.

Many politicians run for something in high school, college, or soon afterward. They get an education and get into walks of life that support their political ambitions.

Like firefighters running into burning buildings to save lives, good politicians want to serve to enable and realize their constituents' sense of possibilities. They show astuteness at balancing politics with their role as public servants. They lead others.

Along the way, their political acumen and showmanship will be revealed to learned eyes. People who know them well will know their interest in politics. Usually, there are no surprises for childhood buddies. Of course, few people are born politicians; many gain the skills through nurture.

If politics is your passion, start early in your local organizations—neighborhood, high school, college, and workplace. Showcase yourself as a leader; connect with people with know-how.

If you have lot of ideas, but no money, influence, or connections, your political dream may collapse like a sandy castle on the beach. Working with elected officials as an apprentice or on a political campaign is a common pathway for those dreaming of holding political office. The trick is building connections early and honing skills to favor diplomacy. Understand the importance of relationships—and do your best to be seen by the right political players.

Astute politicians know how to talk grassroots and steer politics away from electoral laws. They coin catchy buzzwords to make their points or shock the system. They have strategic communications that addresses truth and lie machines and media problems. They monitor the incumbents they want to replace while keeping an eye on other competitors. If the political situation is standing still, they make a move to fill it. They will float trial balloons as an alternative choice to the status quo. They often profess to be a change maker—someone who will make a difference.

Political calculus favors politicians who push for progress more than total change. Voters are reluctant to buy into revolutionary change unless it is an idea whose time has come, which can withstand and survive a hurricane. In such a situation, once the incumbent's domino starts to fall, they fall quickly.

Consider evolutionary changes first. When people want change, they can tolerate gradual change better than radical change. Either way, things will never be the same. There will be a new normal for people to accept and live with. It can be traumatic for some people. It is best to prioritize your evolution. You cannot take on the whole world with a bite, but you can take on selected muscle movements one after another.

Many politicians say their cause is a movement, and they will work within the system, work around the system, or disrupt the system to turn probabilities into possibilities. Many politicians are very good at promises—and very good at keeping none or only a few. Some politicians only affect things at the margins. Very limited numbers of politicians say something and have the goods to back it up. Many voters see politician as all talk and no action. That statement is not all inclusive. Most politicians find political victories intoxicating and will go to any length to extend their terms. If you poll voters, many will scoff at politicians being careerist—staying past their welcome in the protected political bubble or hopping from one political job to another without going back into the real world. Many politicians tend to lose touch with reality as they age. Politics is a supersized profession, and it demands a personality that is possessed by only a few.

It is common for political rivalries to shoot the horse before taking on the rider. Although family or personal life used to be off-limits, that is not the case anymore. It is the actual attack point.

Many would-be politicians, afraid of their privacy implosion, drop out as fast as they jumped into the race. If you have a skeleton in your closet, expect it to be part of the public discourse—and expect some sharp elbows.

Politicians know political debate is stage-craft performance, and they try to outshine their opponents when the limelight is on them. Timely witty responses and interjections tend to make post-debate media headlines and garner political experts' pontifications. They are on the lookout for any opportunity to land a blow. They want to secure the last laugh.

At debate preparations, it would make sense to craft buzzwords or story lines to key points by topics. They use buzzwords and snippy counterarguments, and if time permits, they launch new attacks. With good preparation, you will not be forced to fight on your back foot.

Audience debate fatigue comes to bear when candidates show a lack of command of relevant facts or have low performance and personality quotients.

When politicians speak evasively, opponents counterattack, call out the nonanswers, and expand on the gaps with questions. Astute politicians tend to have ready-made questions for opponent's perceived weak points. The ultimate goal is to exploit opportunities and weaken opponents while making the case that they are better.

It is not uncommon to see politicians employ disinformation to emotionally hijack or demoralize the other side into political convulsions. It is not uncommon to see politicians besiege voters with a tornado of fake news via multifaceted media platforms. Some politicians use campaign messages at rallies to direct and coordinate their attack tactics. They want to undermine their opponents. Some politicians outsource their corrosive deeds. They tend to be excellent at explaining away the controversial deeds because they are mercurial. They claim to have no knowledge of the matter in question or say they are not the same person they were yesterday. Who is? Fortunately, obstruction of justice still keeps the slick politicians in hot water.

If you look around, it does not take long to see politicians' hypocrisy in the naked form. It is very hard to find pure morality in politics. In politics, intellectual honesty and consistency are in short supply.

Some politicians remain patriotic to the core and are truly honorable. Given the opportunity to be a politician, be one of those honorable patriots.

◆ ◆ ◆

Understanding the layers of government would improve your insight of the political landscape. It all cascades from the nation's Constitution, form of government, political parties, and governance. The chosen political power, driven by the chosen economic system, influences governance. Ultimately, the way the governed feel is ruled in or ruled out by national, state, and local policies. The nation's Constitution is the blueprint for how its government works. The Constitution provides fundamental principles and governing structure, and it determines expressed and implied powers, which provide the basis for governance.

Take a quick look at three of the main forms of government: government by many, government by a singular authority, and government by a few.

Government by many is democracy. The key principle is power belongs to the people or power by the people for the people. It is seen as a representative government where eligible citizens cast their votes to pick representatives by the way of a simple majority or electoral votes. Another core principle is division of power for balance of power. Three government branches (executive, legislative, and judiciary) are in place to check on each other. An inability to build consensus among them can delay or prevent necessary actions.

Government by singular authority is monarchy. The key principle is a single individual personifies power, and government is singular authority. This individual comes from the same bloodline from generation to generation.

Government by a few is an oligarchy. The key principle is power belongs to the wealthy and powerful people.

No matter the form of government, dictatorial and autocratic tendencies tend to raise their ugly heads when the governing leaders wield and exert power to repress groups of citizens. Authoritarians succeed by eroding democracy, which puts question marks on the illusion of democracy.

Being familiar with the dominant economic drivers (capitalism, communism, and socialism) will help your efforts to put your arms around how the government machines operate.

Capitalism is free enterprise: freedom to privately own properties and businesses; compete with each other as motivated by profit; and operate in compliance with government regulations in lawful production and services. Supply and demand determine price, but the government intervenes to prevent runaway prices, price fixing, hoarding, and other impediments. Workers' right and upward mobility are parts of the internal mechanism. Generally, enterprises are not under government control.

Communism embraces public and government ownership and government control of chosen industries. The people share the benefit of labor and receive things they "need" from the government. Communism attempts to have a classless society.

Socialism entails public ownership and common control within the government systems. The government regulates everything and encourages cooperation within the government and no competition. Socialism exists in overall system or within factions of an industry. Production and distribution of goods and services are shared. Government tends to promote egalitarian society—commitment to societal equality for all people. The government typically controls prices.

In the twenty-first century, pure economic drivers are no longer common practices. In many nations, you will find a combination of economic drivers. An offshoot of capitalism is a mixed market system, which allows nation-state-supported industries without impeding or preventing free enterprise. Privatization reigns. In other words, freedom to compete and offer choices remain, and the government does not own the market. State-funded universities and postal services are typical examples.

Next is the role of the government at the federal and state levels. The government's foremost role is protecting its sovereignty—political stability and security. The federal government has central powers—some of which are expressed, and some are implied. Common among them include raising military and declaring war;

regulating commerce and overseeing trades between states and other countries; making money; and managing foreign relations. The concurrent powers of the federal and state governments include making and enforcing laws, levying taxes, borrowing money, running the courts, and spending and borrowing power. Some other responsibilities are unspoken, and some evolve with time. Examples include establishing clean air and water, free kindergarten to high school education, social security, and the Affordable Care Act health insurance.

State government powers conserve the lives, liberty, and property of her people. The state has police power. The state manages public health and welfare. The state oversees trade in the state and ratifies federal constitutional amendments.

States cannot block federal laws enacted by Congress. When states have conflicts with the federal government, except on the grounds of unconstitutional law, the federal power tends to override or preempt. When states or federal government feel the other is overreaching or grabbing power, either may resort to court challenges.

Local governments and cities are the states' contact points where the rubber meets the road and where the monies are made doing the heavy-duty lifting. They deliver modern amenities for everyday living—in urban, suburban, metropolitan, and rural areas. They promote and implement policies for property and people's safety and civil rights. They execute law enforcement through local police with state and federal judicial resources. Based on jurisdiction, they prosecute through the state or federal court systems.

Infrastructure and amenities that local governments and cities offer make the difference in the quality of life enjoyed by the people. A quick rundown of the offerings may be appropriate.

Cheap access to utilities (electricity, water, gas, sewage, and garbage). Central water drainage and sanitation management is the practice.

They enable residential real estate from rowhouses to skyscraper flats and single-housing units. Also available are retail and office spaces to include mixed-use development zones.

Yes, zone industrial cluster—manufacturing establishments with complementary logistics, learning, and research centers.

Also, there are industrial farming and fisheries that feed the state, nation, and more.

They ensure hospitals, clinics, and tertiary medical establishments are part of the infrastructure package.

They ensure banks, post offices, public libraries, fuel stations, and other vital facilities are readily available.

They ensure museums, art galleries, amusement parks, cinema and concert theaters, community centers, health clubs, movie and music studios, places of worship, and day care centers are in place to serve local communities.

They ensure availability of public parks and public areas for recreation—even dog parks, festival arenas, and reenactment centers.

They preserve historic districts and neighborhoods, iconic buildings like castles and church cathedrals, revered sites with monuments and memorials, and symbolic structures like the Statue of Liberty and Eiffel Tower.

They ensure availability of nature trails for bikers, runners, and walkers; and nature preserves like botanical gardens and zoos. Bodies of water, beaches, and riverfront developments are features in the amenities package.

They ensure land-use planning encourages area beautification and creative use of vacant land with active forest management. They foster a sense of community with vegetation, which promotes clean environment.

They ensure shopping centers, department stores, and grocery stores are available. Shopping plazas give patrons a nostalgic air of freedom and access to retail shop and merchandise. Pedestrian malls, retail shops, and street food vendors offer authentic cuisine. Open markets include neighborhood farmers markets and vendor markets.

They promote downtown and town squares with lighted main streets, city centers with sidewalks, shops, and restaurants, urban metered parking stands, and public parking garages. They include vibrant streets with bars and clubs to nurture nightlife.

Local governments and cities support hotels with budget to luxury accommodations, and resorts in prime locations. These hotels have spaces for cultural attractions.

Restaurant alleys offer specialty meals from indigenous to Asian, Spanish, and European cuisines. Food is served with unique fanfare: American burgers and toppings, Italian pizzas with toppings, tacos and burritos, steaks, schnitzel, fried rice, rolled-up African fufu, bowls of spicy soup, and more.

The locations of top fast-food chains and specialty restaurants are based upon market demand. Mobile food trucks and street food vendors fill the needs of people on the go. States promote ethnic, holiday dish menus, and authentic cuisines.

Through the local governments and cities, the state and the nation promote literacy through their school systems. In the United States, kindergarten to twelfth grade (elementary, middle, and high school) is free in the public education system. At the postsecondary and postgraduate levels, students pay out of pocket. In some Northern European nations with very high adult literacy, the entire education system is supported by the state with free tuition for citizens. Could that be a good example for the world?

Through the local governments and cities, the state and the nation support different sports. Their entertainment offerings include sports venues, football fields, baseball fields, hockey rinks, racetracks, track and field stadiums, and golf courses. They adopt and endorse sports and athletic activities to match tradition and culture. The major sports culminate in professional leagues. The National Collegiate Athletic Association regulates student-athlete programs, which serve as feeders for professional leagues and breeding grounds for Olympic athletes.

Becoming an Olympian, particularly a medalist, requires world-class excellence. Also, being a professional in any sport can lead to money and fame.

Through the local governments and cities, the state and the nation enable information flow. The battle for freedom of speech plays out daily in the individual rights and mass media fronts. Independent TV networks, radio stations, newspaper outlets, and digital and social media platforms flood society with information as they compete for attention. Individuals and groups often ruffle the government's feathers. Governments do not kill citizens for what they say. The nations' constitutions require the government to have tolerance for freedom of speech.

Through local governments and cities, the state and the nation contribute to establishing a transportation network. They provide serviceable roads with easy access to state and federal highways.

Through the local governments and cities, the state and the nation contribute to the conditions that enable private automobile ownership to more than 50 percent of eligible adults.

Infrastructure gives access to public transit carriers. Bus transit includes local lines and city hop-on, hop-off buses. Rental cars, ride-share programs, and taxi services are available. At tourist hubs, horse carriage rides are available.

Civilian airports and airlines are in service within an hour of metropolitan areas.

A rail network is part of the solution: cargo trains, commuter rail lines, and light-rail cars. Altogether, the system delivers a first-class transportation network for people, freight, and commerce. Because of the great efforts of good politicians and other individuals running the various government-interdependent systems, these amenities appear to be on autopilot. Great local governments and cities post high-quality infrastructure and amenities that provide a high quality of life. They earn five-star reviews when compared to failed states' amenities.

The world's advanced nations, states, local governments, and cities understand the importance of living life and enabling it. Locales with high standards of living tend to have amenities that operate like they are made by nature and not by humans. Their environments draw residents and visitors who want to explore the experiences they offer.

The above list is not all-inclusive, and no single nation or state has a monopoly on perfect infrastructure and amenities or all the ideas to improve them. That is why some places are grander than others.

◆ ◆ ◆

Government revenues and expenditures are an important facet of governance. Most governments generate revenue through income taxes (individual and corporate), consumption taxes (sales, value added tax, and exercise), property taxes (initial, recurring, and transfer), and charges and fees from imports, exports, and services. Wealth taxes are collected in some places.

Tax systems in advanced nations can be tricky to navigate. In some nations, the average take-home pay is in the sixtieth percentile. Some nations and states have no personal income taxes, but they utilize other tax vehicles to gain revenues. Some have fiscal policies that make them tax havens for rich individuals and businesses.

Who collects what taxes and from whom? Some of the taxes are collected at the federal level, and some are collected at the state and city levels. How equitable is the tax system? Is it progressive? How efficient is the tax-collection system? Is the government running a deficit or a surplus? Is the effective tax rate pro-business or not? In my opinion, the overall effective tax rate should never exceed 20 percent. What is taxed and at what rate affects businesses and people. How can the government raise revenue? Where do its expenditures go? That is homework for the politicians.

◆ ◆ ◆

Next is the global indexes. A global index secures independent local data on key factors and uses standardized metrics and methodologies to describe, score, and rank nations. This information provides insights into the health of a country when compared to other nations.

A lot of indexes exist, but my favorites include the Human Development Index by country at United Nations Development Programme (measures key dimensions of human development), the Corruption Perception Index at Transparency International (provides corruption level perception by the public), the World Justice Project Rule of Law Index from World Justice Project (captures rule of law experience and perception of the public) and the Quality of Life Indexes (purchasing power, safety, health care, cost of living, property price to income, traffic commute time, pollution, and climate) at Numbeo. These give insights into the well-being of a country. Fortunately, these indexes are accessible online.

Do not forget to take a peek at the independent educational websites—like World Top Export—which present the latest export news, trends, and opportunities, and are designed to inspire researchers around the globe. Tons of information is available when you search the internet for best independent educational website for political candidates.

If your country, state, and city scores and rankings are not among the best, why not? You can identify the areas that need improvements and come up with agendas to improve them. You can learn from those who have across-the-board excellence.

More advanced nations tend to rank favorably on most indexes. Most of them excel at multiple industries, which include industrial products manufacturing, consumer goods production, agricultural production, technology, tourism, and services. They export these things.

Nations with the best ratings tend to have public policies that serve their high socioeconomic life. Also, their foreign relations go beyond just being members of the United Nations, International Monetary Fund, World Bank, World Trade Organization, continental and regional blocs, Group of Seven, Group of Twenty, and intergovernmental political forums. These nations hold respectable places in the world market and keep the world order.

A poor global index ranking is a red cluster indicator. It points to inherent problems that need urgent attention. What is the cause of the problems? Government power structure? Governance accountability? Ideology? Is it regulations and taxes? Is it population or worker efficiency? Is the solution economic freedom and civil liberty? You be the judge.

The nations with the lowest indexes post the greatest trade deficits because they are indebted to advanced nations and state. What can you do to make what is bad good, good better, or better best?

Do regions of the world and their unique climates (tropical, temperate, dry, cold, and polar) set the stage for where they end up? Adaptation means the more, the better.

◆ ◆ ◆

Keep your eye on the ball. Who you vote into power and what they stand for and do will determine the fate of the society you live in. Vote for leaders who will do the right things in the right ways. They must know there are consequences for every political decision. They must find solutions and understand that today's solutions might be tomorrow's problems. No matter what, they must take the required actions now and append their labor of love signature with pride.

Yes, politics is a strategy and not an ideology. Be smart. Do not make yourself absent. Be present and be felt. If you cannot beat them, join the best of two evils. Take your seat at the table of the human race and make your political impact.

Is your dream to be a politician and change the world? Way to go. Jump in. What are your gifts, talents, and strengths? Match opportunities to your talents. Explore and exploit them.

Start with where you are and with what you have. Do what you can. Be honest with yourself. You cannot be everything or do everything. Do not let your opinion hold you hostage. Only fools do that. Take advice from mentors and wise folks—and change your mind if you need to.

It makes sense to develop your mindset to be a public servant and have your priorities right before running for anything political. Your private life will be set up for public spectacle. Watch the incumbent politicians for their waxing and waning periods. Go in at low tide or flatline. Timing is everything. At the right moment, you will have a fighting chance.

Politics is a team sport. Neglect joining a winning team at your peril. If you do not like what is going on and do not want to be silent or complicit, do something. Do not let perfect be the enemy of the good. If accountability is lacking, the incumbent is vulnerable. Flawed character and broken promises could be a trigger point to enter the political arena. Assess how people feel. Your chances of succeeding increase if the likability factor is in your favor.

Define your political positions by isolating what is in and what is out. Determine what you must include and what you must exclude. You may be as visionary as you want, but fixing the people's day-to-day needs come first. Focus and work on the things people care about.

Talk and embrace a forward-looking agenda. Call out your opponent's agenda as backward, which time has passed. Underplay the incumbent's strength and overplay their weaknesses. Exploit the gaps and redefine your opponent's platforms and policies to your advantage. Expose the incumbent's priorities, money allocations, and relationships.

Define existing problems and offer fresh solutions. Frame the incumbent as the problem or part of the problem. Frame questions about the situation with catchy phrases. Make case for why change is needed followed with solutions with catchy phrases. Persuasive and inspirational politicians tend to have it easier in winning over a crowd.

A good communication strategy could be to under-promise and over-deliver with objectives to match. Write down your objectives and verbally reiterate them to bring them to life. Yes, at the critical time period, have the story of the day, the week, and the month.

Be aware that voter suppression and dissuasion are in play. Gerrymandering and redistricting can dilute or strengthen a group to favor those in power. Electoral subversion and disruption are increasing and becoming arrows in politics.

In your opposition research, assemble the incumbent's derogatory and controversial statements and negative assessments from people who knew them. Weaponize the information to undo your opponent, drop bombshells, and wind up the public's anticipation for the next shoe to drop.

Build a political machine for fundraising, running, and winning. Voters have mixed feelings on the role of corporate sponsorships. Politicians rely on people who been there and done it. Hire an experienced staff.

Learn to avoid unforced errors. Don't run a braggadocious campaign. Engage potential contenders and see if you can persuade them to suspend their candidacy and support you.

Always speak tactfully and diplomatically because your past statements can be used to discount you. Do not just fight against something—fight *for* something. Narrative matters.

Do not offer opinions on controversial issues you are not qualified to speak on, such as the Holocaust. Educate yourself on such matters first.

It seems like politicians go to school to answer questions. Sometimes, they give no answers and revert to canned responses. Sometimes, they simply choose not to answer the question. Sometimes, they pawn off the question as something they would rather not comment on. Sometimes, they try to turn the question around. Other times, they may say they are not in a position to answer the question, but here's what they can say. Astute politicians, in a very polite manner, leverage open-ended questions to tell their stories. Many politicians give one- or two-word responses when they do not like the question.

Be prepared for your opponents' attacks. As you are looking into them, they will be looking into you. You will feel like you live in a glass house. Many of your opponents will make efforts to see through you. Be vigilant and watch out for false flag. Nip them in the bud. Know how not to fight on your back foot. You have nothing to fear if you are ethical and grounded. If you win, be humble and reach out to the opposition. Be careful not to overestimate your mandate. The first advantage you give your opponent is to underestimate them. If you lose, be gracious. When the election is over, get together to see what can be done in a bipartisan manner. If you dabble in politics, be ready for a brawl. Don't be discouraged by what your opponents say or do. A flat tire can hinder a trip, but it will not stop the journey. A smooth path leads to nowhere important. Behind big obstacles, there are big chances. Do not give up before you succeed. There are no excuses and no surrender. Reach out and grab your destiny.

PART III

BUILDING WEALTH

GG's second pillar of life is building wealth. Having the right job is crucial. Owning your own house—or other property—is important too. Having sensible savings and investments while optimizing and leveraging your credit scores and actuarial coverages are part of the solution.

CHAPTER 12

THE RIGHT JOB

GG says there are many fishes in the ocean, but you will be hungry until you catch one. Even for low-hanging fruit, you may still need a ladder to reach it. It takes work to get the right job, and you may get into your dream occupation by accident.

After graduation from high school or college, anxiety and fear about being on your own for the first time will be real. Your first real job, exposure to workplace politics, first apartment, first car, paying your own bills, and a new romance can be scary feeling. That is all OK. No worries. Some feel-good moments will come when you see progress and accomplishments.

If you know your passion and strengths, you can go into career that gives you satisfaction and makes you feel fulfilled. You need a job to survive—and to thrive. Earning a good income will make you feel financially liberated. Money can buy you a lot of things. There are many things money cannot buy, but with more money, you have more options.

Do your homework on what your targeted employers or customers want. Prepare yourself for the work environment where you have to display maturity and be accountable to others.

Have a work-life plan. Expect reality to square off with your expectations. Pick a walk of life.

The importance of knowing what you want to be and having a road map to get you there is invaluable.

As a teen, you may be unsettled about your vocation of choice. Your parents' role in preparing and shaping your life cannot be in mute mode. Your parents know your likes, dislikes, and potential from their close-up daily observations. It is your parents' duty to talk to you about the different vocations in life. That discussion may include examples from real life, books, TV, movies, travel, sports, or stories. By any means possible, your parents should try to expose you to the possibilities of a life that is worthy of working for.

Children's books are a good introduction to different walks of life. If you are gifted in science, reading science books and watching science programs will be beneficial. The same thing applies to other fields of study. Your parents may encourage you to be a comedian, a musician, a lawyer, a doctor, a professor, a nurse, an engineer, or an entrepreneur. There is nothing wrong with your parents wanting you to be the greatest of all time in something. As a matter of fact, it is a duty that your parents owe you.

As a teenager, if you know exactly what you want and commit to excelling in it, you will be head and shoulders above your peers. Be that teenager. What do you yearn for? Is being an entrepreneur your goal? Are jobs in the commercial sector interesting? Is a job in the religious field your calling? What about federal or state government jobs where years of service tend to be transferrable and carried over from one job to another?

Consider jobs in financial services; medical and health services; logistics; entertainment; news; technology and digital fields; education or academia; engineering; business services; law enforcement; military; judiciary; manufacturing; consumer services; sports; and professional specialties in science and arts. Military service and law enforcement are hidden gems, but they are not for everyone. Teachers are among the most educated, yet their pay lags. However, many teachers have unmatched job satisfaction. Do your research because there are plenty of good-paying jobs out there. Pick the right industry, career field, and occupation for you. It's not bad to become an entrepreneur and be your own boss and employ others.

One of the main reasons for having a job is earning a good income. Money will give you the freedom to buy whatever money can buy. The more dollars you have, the more options you have. Hopefully, you are happy making the dollars. Money does not guarantee happiness, but with a good income, many things are possible, including building wealth.

A good job pays off in financial and benefit packages. You must work hard to prepare yourself for a good job and stay alert for the opportunity when it comes.

Making money requires talent, skills, taking risks, and being in the right job in the right place at the right time.

Show passion for the vocation of your choice. If you do, it will help you see your worst workday with an optimistic lens. You will look at what you have and see it as more because something is better than nothing. You will turn uncertainty into hope. No matter what job you have, there will be easy days and hard days. Being optimistic helps.

A key to success is perseverance. You must know when to dig deep to weather the storm, survive to fight another day, or head for the higher ground. Everything that goes wrong is not your fault; some things are beyond your control. You will rarely get bored with what you love to do. Feed the beast in you by aiming high and getting a college education in your area of passion before jumping into the workforce full-time.

A college degree is no longer a guaranteed ticket to a good job, but without it, your chances take a hit. A college degree is a stepping stone; it is a universal certification that you can perform common tasks beyond a high school level. Without the certification, some opportunities and jobs may be unavailable to you. A societal norm is that all young people need to get a college education. Those who don't wish they did, and they sometimes feel left out. Try not to shortchange yourself. Get a college degree or learn a trade before you take on other life responsibilities, particularly marriage and having kids.

Once you get into a job that suits your interest, invest your energy and time, and learn from the best. Believe in yourself. Give your chosen walk of life your best effort every day. Shoot to be above average in all you do, but never twist yourself into pretzel while doing that. Do not be a prophet of doom. Remember that daylight comes after the darkness.

Work hard to be above average and among the best. If you do, you will have a great chance of being recognized and rewarded handsomely. March to the beat of your own drummer, but look at the planting season and harvesting season for what they are. Each season will demand your best efforts if you want a productive yield. Work hard each season if you want a good harvest. It is better to have and not need than to need and not have. The time to think about tomorrow's season is not tomorrow; it was yesterday and many days earlier.

Own your decision—and forgive yourself if you cannot see the fine line between excellence and perfection. The key is to be fully prepared, hold the shield in your nondominant hand, and be ready. With some good luck, the opportunity will come your way to strike your saber on the target and get your dream job.

It will be great to have a job that gives you happiness, allows you to contribute and make an impact on your family, community, and the world, and touch people for good. The sun is not there to cast shadows; sunlight is there to serve as our best disinfectant.

Your unique footprint, if placed correctly, will help others find their way long after you are gone. Success leaves footprints.

Dream big. Let your imagination run wild because you can be anything you want to be with some helping hands. It is OK to dream and aspire to do better than your parents. Many parents truly want their kids to be successful and be in the middle class or top earners. What you do with the dream will seal your faith in being a dreamer or a top earner.

One bad decision can change the course of your life and take you to the bottom of the mountain. Similarly, one good decision can blast your door open to stardom. You have many paths in life to take. The one you take is your choice. You will reap the benefits or live the natural consequences of the choices you make. Be careful.

No matter where your starting point is, living on the margins after college should not make you less than anyone else. The fact that you hold a job dignifies you as a responsible person. Be proud of yourself. You are not a rolling stone that gathers no moss.

However, well-paying jobs will rarely come to you; you have to go to them. If success does not come to you, you should go to it. Persevere in looking for a better-paying career and not just a job. If that ship does not come in, you can swim to it with enthusiasm and commitment. In your job search, start with what you know and want. Which rich neighborhoods do you want to live in? What kind of jobs do people who live there do? Bingo. Whatever vocations they have pay enough to enable them to live there. You should seek similar jobs.

Choose industries that cover the jobs you believe your targeted income earners work in and research them. Internet search engines like Google are your friends. Use them to zero in on occupations that will pay well and provide job satisfaction. Peel back the layers to find statistics on career progression rate, benefit packages, and other things.

Many good companies proudly post their industry recognitions, awards, and more on their websites. It is important to pay attention to the recognition dates. Some companies will be in decline. There is no one-stop shop to find information about your company of interest. Ask for information from anyone who can help. Connect or network with anyone who can open doors for you.

Some job boards provide relevant information on job availability, pay range, and what to expect of the job. Enhance your job search awareness with websites like LinkedIn, Indeed, Glassdoor, and ZipRecruiter.

The US Bureau of Labor Statistics, www.bls.gov, can provide tons of information about current and future job outlooks, industry profiles, and more. Look for the jobs of the future—not just for today—and avoid jobs that appear to be going obsolete.

What do employers want? If employers want what they want, you must be what they want to make yourself employable. When a monkey asks for banana, you give the monkey what it wants. Prepare yourself to fit the needs and expectations of your employer. Figure out what your bosses professionally want and give it to them.

There is no alternative to a competent and loyal employee who always wears a warm smile. Make yourself special. Do not just meet deadlines—beat the deadlines. The more proficient you are, the more likely you are to be trusted. Be a man of integrity and make your bosses shine. When your bosses look good, you look good. Be employable.

People like people who like them. Friendliness and warmness are social lubricants. Treat others with respect and kindness. Embrace them. Do unto others as you would have them do unto you. This does not mean being terminally nice or being nice to a fault.

Many people like peers who show passion, enthusiasm, and confidence. They like peers who light up the room with a positive attitude. Your attitude is a choice you make. Show up with an attitude of service and a team spirit that inspires others to do more. Be a team player. Be executive material—and be ready for your time at the helm.

Relationships are dynamic, and people are always changing. What do you do when you are the most powerful person in the room? Remember how you felt on your way up the ladder; your juniors are people and have feelings too.

You are hired. Now what? You will deal with the work environment. You should know that a workplace is a competitive arena. Organizations optimize their limited resources to generate the highest returns on investment and meet their goals.

Expect to work with all kinds of people. Some people want to be the ringside judge all the time. Others enjoy being spectators on the sideline. Some will need sparring partners. Some will take an uppercut and floored—yet be saved by the bell. Some will come out swinging for the fences. Some may win by a nose. Some avoid fumbling the ball and play to win the game as a team. Some will take off the gloves or throw in the towel before the bout starts. Each person may come in with a different agenda, but the work environment shapes the group requirements. Eventually, people find their niches.

Once you are part of the team, you will begin to see the different composition. People and staff positions are different by design. What is your niche? Make yourself a value-added person who is fresh, loyal, and enthusiastic. Do not be the guy who has all the questions and no answers.

When orchestra blends together, it becomes a symphony. There is nothing wrong with expecting a harmonious work environment. However, at times, you might run into sour people.

You will have the option to jump ship or hang in there until they leave the job.

Do not expect white-glove treatment from all the people you encounter. At life's crossroads, you will have to fight for oxygen because many people coming from all directions will intersect, and each person is trying to make their way forward.

You cannot improve or get stronger without challenges. When the going gets tough, the tough get going. They default to their reflex. You must get your act together, own your actions, and persevere. Take your blessings where you find them as you march forward to achieve your destiny. Work to live—and not live to work.

Expect an active work life between twenty-two and seventy years of age. Some seniors work full-time into their seventies and beyond. Seniors, in their eighties, particularly in politics, should be aware that what matters most is no longer their presence in the workforce; the decline of their energy and intellectual acuity is on obvious display. At the back edge in your golden years, it's time to step down. If you do not want to retire, you could become a mentor for younger generations.

During your work life, you will find yourself going through jobs and juggling occupational risks and compensation packages. You may find yourself changing jobs and careers along the way. You might move from the commercial sector to the government sector or become an entrepreneur. The most important thing is to make progress in your vocation of choice. If you love what you do, do it more. Do not forget to use your starting salary target and career salary goals as guides.

Moving from an entry-level position to junior management within four years of being on the job is an attainable goal. Moving into middle management between the fifth and fifteenth year is within the norm. With fifteen years or more of job experience, your eyes should be on senior management.

You must go into a profession that has room for growth and work for organizations with an equitable upward mobility structure. Try to start with a good job—one that has potential for growth and progression. If you want rapid upward mobility, you may have to move from job to job, seeking increased responsibilities as you gain experience.

Work in a job that pays well or move on. If a job with potential for vertical progression and more benefits did not find you, do not hesitate to find it in another organization or city.

Make hay while the sun is shining. Be adventurous and take risks, but be prudent. If you do not risk anything, you risk being docile. By midlife, your annual income target should be to make six times the existing federal minimum wage income. Above average and upper-middle-class earners tend to make many more times the minimum wage income. Comfortable living, here you come. It is not an overnight process. Depending on the currency, you can become a millionaire.

Hustle now, at a younger age, because you can. Mine for off-the-radar opportunities. Take a second job if time permits. If the second job complements your primary job, it's even better.

Consider taking odd jobs. Being a taxi or an Uber driver—working for yourself at your own convenience—is not a bad option. Explore the gig economy to see what works for you.

Consider temporary jobs as a launching pad. Pay your dues in an apprenticeship. If you show an inclination for greatness, people will recognize you. You can always redirect your focus on a good-paying career.

Never accept living paycheck to paycheck with zero margins. Dig a well before you are thirsty. Plant a seed before you are hungry. Improve your balance sheet now—and make more money, spend wisely, and build more discretionary income.

CHAPTER 13

HOUSE

GG says you become a man when you have your own home. As a young man, the time will come for you to move out of your parents' house and make your own home by getting your own house.

Feeling like you are gaining freedom on your own and being in control of your destiny is exhalating until you are reminded that you need to rent a living place or buy a house to make it a reality.

The location, neighborhood price, characteristics and affordability scale will affect your decision. You may have to balance some other variables to make your decision. Rent an apartment or buy a house? For many young adults, renting is the short-term solution.

Within two to ten years of living on your own, if your income and job are stable, buy your first house. You should try to buy your first house in your early work life or near midlife. Your first house should have less than 2,500 square feet of living space and have two to four bedrooms.

Stay in your starter house long enough to build equity or have the price reasonably appreciate. You should have a goal to buy at least two houses in your lifetime. When buying a house, you will hear advice about "location, location, location."

Imagine the neighborhood twenty years in the future. Assess the current health of the shopping centers, school district, crime rate, city amenities, and property taxes. Watch out for job flight, population flight or influx, and demographic changes. Any red flags about the neighborhood deserve your attention.

When you are interested in a neighborhood, visit the area at daytime and at dusk. The types of activities on the street and the cars in the driveways and on the streets will speak volumes. If the neighborhood charges homeowners association fees, expect the fees to rise as the years pass. Is the neighborhood going to be run down or maintained? From the get-go, pick an above average neighborhood. Good neighborhoods tend to have good resale values.

It's good to have an idea of the type of floor plan you want: open or partitioned living room and kitchen, laundry room and master bedroom at the first or second level. Think of where you want wood floors, tile, or carpet. Think about the cabinet layout and colors in the kitchen and bathrooms. Use what you want as the starting point and adjust your requirements based on the available inventory of houses for sale.

Two-story houses are cheaper than one-story buildings of equal square footage. Many standard houses have three or four symmetrical windows looking from the front of the house and a front-view garage. Fancier houses tend to have five or more asymmetrical windows on the front and a side garage.

Think about your lawn size—the bigger the lawn, the more you will mow. A good-looking lawn calls for serious maintenance, watering, weed treatments, and fertilizer. Expect to put in an average of three hours per week for a half-acre's maintenance during the late spring through early fall, which is when grasses grow the fastest.

Buying a house is a big adventure. Depending on your personal situation, plan to spend 15 percent or more of the house value on required expenses, including down payment, closing costs, and agent fees.

You will have options to finance your home loan. The mortgage term of choice is a fixed rate for fifteen or thirty years. I recommend a fifteen-year mortgage if you can afford the increased monthly payments. You may be surprised to know when the fifteen-year payment is compared to thirty-year mortgage monthly payment, it is only few hundred dollars higher. The fifteen-year mortgage will save you tons of money on interest.

If you choose the thirty-year mortgage, depending on your annual percentage rate (APR), the total interest paid can easily surpass 40 percent of the loan. To reduce your total interest, when you can, make extra monthly payments toward your mortgage principal.

In any case, try to get the best finance rate for your situation. Be sure you fully understand your APR. If feasible, buy down the points. The Federal Truth in Lending Act requires lenders to disclose the yearly cost of installment loans. The more you know about the house-buying nuances, the better questions you can ask—and the more useful and impactful answers you will get.

Lenders determine the APR, but borrowers can negotiate the APR. To help you select the most favorable loan, ask the lenders competing for your business for their APR. Be sure there is no early payoff penalty clause in your contract.

On average, the APR ranges from about 3–8 percent. The APR is the original interest rate plus other finance costs: brokers' fees, mortgage insurance, closing costs, loan origination costs, and fees. Because of the add-ons, the APR is normally higher than the quoted interest rate.

An average house purchase process takes forty-five to ninety days. I recommend going through a buying agent to represent you. Pay for an accredited home inspector service, which is necessary to validate condition of house. A home appraisal is another important piece. It is an authoritative statement on the worth of your house, which is required by the mortgage guarantor. These tertiary services may seem expensive initially, but they are worth every penny to help you have a happy home. Do your homework to get the best service provider in each case.

Do not forget relocation expenses. Your household goods must move from your old house to the new one. Expect move-in expenses (furniture, fittings, utilities, etc.). It's good to have outdoor and indoor security cameras for peace of mind. Consider all these cash requirements when you are considering a house purchase.

When you are still paying your mortgage, if interest rates drop by one or more points from your existing APR, consider refinancing your mortgage. Higher interest rates mean more expensive debt. Take advantage of lower interest rates.

Expect to recover your refinancing costs in about four years. Savings from the interest rate reduction will shave years off your mortgage payoff date, assuming you commit to paying the same amount monthly.

Be familiar with a mortgage amortization calculator. You can access it online at Bankrate.com or calculator.net. Use it to determine your refinance break-even point and then decide if refinancing is worthwhile given your loan time horizon.

The satisfaction of being a homeowner is surreal. It is like being happy for having a college degree—but concerned about your lingering student loan. It is like marriage, which is admitted by many as very hard work, yet many people strive to be married. That is like the euphoria of homeownership.

Homeownership is core facet of American dream. All things being equal, the longer you stay in your first house, the more equity you will build. Selling your first house will enable you to buy outright or finance less money when buying your second home.

Draw from the experiences gained from your first homeownership as you plan to get your second house, which should be your dream home. If you have a wife and kids, you should move to your second home just before your kids are teens and in a position to enjoy their parents' success—and before they head off to college and find their own footing in life. Kids want to remember their rooms before they left home. It's like a museum to their lives. Leave some keepsakes in the room to immortalize it. Whenever your adult kids visit, they will reminiscence and glorify the memories of old times in their rooms and your house. That is priceless.

You have become a man when you own your own house. You can build wealth by owning properties. It takes time and deliberate effort.

CHAPTER 14

SAVINGS AND INVESTMENTS

According to GG, the amount you save and invest count more than what you squander. At a minimum, basic working knowledge of personal finance is essential for building and managing your wealth. You should learn and understand the impact of having idle cash, return on investments, tax-efficient measures, and credit efficiency. Also, early aversion to debt is a habit that is worthy of cultivation.

Choose sensible, frugal living, but do not be foolish frugal. Don't buy what you do not need simply because it is on sale. Pinching pennies here and there on a do-it-yourself project that remains unfinished forever is not frugal. Spending irrationally that leads to waste is not frugal.

Learn to maximize your discretionary savings. Put away resources in aggressive investment vehicles with the possibility of earning fat returns.

When you are young, savings is not on the top of your to-do list. For many, lifestyle inflation rules the day. Impulse buying is another culprit. Unless you are super rich, extravagant and ostentatious living will bury you deep in debt or lead to crime.

Good budgeting is the bedrock of making savings a point of duty. Write down your monthly expenses. Group the expenses into two buckets: necessities and discretionary. Your goal should be to keep expenses under 60 percent of your income. Put the remaining 40 percent of your income into savings and investment—25 percent in savings and 75 percent in investment vehicles of your choice. Be mindful of low interest rates on savings accounts and the impact of inflation on cash.

Why do you need to save and invest? For targeted purchases, rainy days, and financial peace of mind. Even ants and squirrels stock up for rainy days. In case you need inspiration, the best savers have a net worth of more than ten times their highest annual salary by their late sixties. The minimum investment net worth target at sixty should be six times your highest annual salary; at fifty, five times; at forty, four times; and at thirty, more than one times your annual pay. You can be one of the best savers. Start to save early and aggressively invest as much as possible. You get the point.

The importance of starting savings early and investing wisely cannot be overemphasized. Do not forget to increase your savings and investment rate as your earnings grow and as you are able to cut back on your monthly bills. Have you considered living in an inexpensive city?

It is important to open and maintain a checking account to run your expenses and a regular savings account to hold your reserve of three to six months of expenses. Bouncing checks is a cardinal sin. Never write a check when you do not have the cash in your bank account to pay it. Since money-transfer apps like Zelle, Cash, Venmo, and PayPal have taken over, writing checks is now an old-school exercise. Avoid overdraft fees on your accounts. No matter how much you make, if you spend more than you make, you are in deep kimchi. You must be savvy with your money to build wealth. Your income-to-expense ratio is important. Do not spend more than you budget or earn.

Explore and capitalize on the power of comparative online shopping. Various apps can help you save money. Join Honey app is one of the best. It automatically finds great deals at checkout. Raise.com is great for discounted gift cards. Use RetailMeNot to find discount codes. To be among the first to know about deals, you may sign up for daily or weekly email updates with sales flyers from your favorite stores and brands.

For food and home goods, if you do not shop in wholesale clubs, like Costco or Sam's Club, you are leaving your discounts on the table. Check out Amazon for whatever deals are available too.

Do not go shopping for food when you are hungry. Everything will look appetizing, and you might want it all. Hungry shopping is dangerous for your wallet.

To avoid sellers taking you on a sales gimmick ride, have general knowledge of items' selling price.

Buy one get one free does not mean it's cheap. The price could have been raised for the first item. Nothing is free. A rat that does not know there is no free cheese gets caught. If you are not paying for the product, you are the product. Some sellers mark up prices and promise a discount, which will bring the item back to the original selling price. You must have an idea about the general cost of items to help you confirm the so-called sales items are really on sale.

Take truth in pricing with a grain of salt. It is best to pay a discounted price that is lower than the manufacturer's suggested retail price.

Price haggling is not a sin, but you need to know where and when to haggle. It is done in many parts of the world.

If your plan is maximum deals, try to buy a few weeks before the end of the season. At the right time, you can easily find items at bargain prices—even 50 percent or more discounts. Be aware that selections may be limited.

Buy trendy clothes in season to feel good. Buy quality, but buy less. Use the stuff you bought longer before discarding it. Mix up your clothes with three-quarters conservative clothes and a quarter trendy clothes.

Take advantage of holiday discounts. A great time for online bargain hunting is a week or two before major holidays. You will notice best deals and good merchandise selections compared to the actual holiday. Take advantage of national holidays, Black Friday discounts, and Cyber Monday sales. Do not forget that big brands and chain stores often have discount days. Shop the deep discounts during end-of-season sales.

When you shop for deals, consider the day of the week. Wednesdays and Thursdays are best for groceries. If savings is your thing, arrange vacation travel early and off-season. Similarly, buy seasonal goods at deep discounts. During end-of-season blowout sales, retailers are making room for the new season's offerings. If the merchandise does not serve a practical purpose and fill your need, forget it. If you practice that, you will not have buyer's remorse.

You can negotiate for lower rates at the start and at contract renewal of your utility services (gas, electricity, water, trash, cable TV, internet, and phone). Go online and research rates. Equipped with that information, contact the utility service providers and ask for their best discounts for existing or new customers. Get quotes for one- or two-year service arrangements. Compare local providers' service rates and select the best value.

If you are running into headwinds, ask for the company's customer loyalty or retention department. You will be amazed by how you can stretch your savings in reoccurring bills just by asking.

For your banking services, do not overlook credit unions. They provide banking services at lower costs.

If you are in the market for a car, ask for the out-the-door price. Auto dealers have ways of getting you to pay a premium besides the asking price. You may cut the chase by offering an out-of-the door price. If your bid is fair, the dealer will likely accommodate you with some minor number plays. After all, auto dealers are itching to make sales, which will be a win-win for both parties. Outgoing models are discounted when the new models arrive and immediately after auto shows feature redesigned models. Knowing the timeline of the vehicle of your interest and leveraging it can save you money.

Try to avoid life mistakes like divorce and crime; in some form or shape, they will affect your finances. Divorce, particularly when kids are involved, will forever unravel you and your family's emotional bedrock. The financial pain is fresh in the minds of those involved. Crime—petty or hardcore, is a stain on your character, and it will follow you for the rest of your life. You might never be in position to tally the full costs.

It is noble to help others, but do not overextend yourself financially. It can take more than just one person to pull up the person who fell off the cliff. It takes people to support a village, and villages can support a town. Know your place.

Try to manage your spending habits and balance needs versus wants before pulling the trigger. You must get that horse in check before it comes out of the barn. Strive to live a debt-free life and aggressively invest some of your income.

Try to get cheap interest rates if you have to buy on credit. For retail purchases with credit cards, the interest rate ranges from about 10 percent to mid-20s. Generally, the interest rate you pay is determined by lenders using the prevailing government prime rate and your credit score. Borrowers who have higher credit scores receive better rates.

It is wise to save for most things you buy and to pay when you buy. It is best to pay off your credit card charges each month. Buy what you need before you buy what you want. Never overlook the financial cost of ownership for whatever you buy and the time you will put in attending to whatever it is. Cut your coat according to your size. As you make your bed, you will lie on it.

If you must carry over credit card debt balances from one month to another, make on-time payments. Do not get behind on your payments. No delinquency, period. Expect to bear the immense burden of compounding interest on your unpaid debt balances. Creditors will hold you accountable for blowing up your credit.

For installment loans, seriously consider additional payments toward the loan principal each month. By doing so, you will be guaranteed an earlier payoff date and reduce the total interest paid. Ultimately, you will save and keep more of your money for yourself instead of giving it away to lenders as interest payments.

Investing in market securities will help grow your wealth. If you understand the security market, a do-it-yourself approach may work for you. Passive investment portfolios like index funds are doable. If you find investing intimidating, try a financial management service.

A good financial advisor will guide you through the minefield, match your investment goals, and find a risk-tolerance level for your investment capital allocation (stocks, mutual funds, and bonds). They will help you make timely adjustments during market volatility.

Invest for the long haul. The stock market is risky business, and market volatility is real and not for the faint of heart. Betting on the economy is a loser's game. Market speculation and timing can be a disaster for amateurs because you must be right twice: knowing when to buy and when to sell. Buying or selling on emotion is a disaster. The market's boom-and-bust cycles swing irregularly. It can seem like there is no rhyme or reason when it come to market activities. No day is business as usual because something on one end of the world can trigger an avalanche in the market. Buy low, sell high is a mantra, but the right gauge point can be elusive for an average investor.

Think about short- and long-term investments. Be conservative in the short term and aggressive with your long-term investments. Have a balanced portfolio. Leave your brokerage account management to the professionals. You will need a reputable brokerage company to manage your portfolio. Consider the company's investment-expense ratio and the particular investment running rate of returns. High-turnover investment holdings and frequent buying and selling of investments can trigger fees and taxes, which may reduce your fund's performance. Do not forget management fees; they all add up. Be smart. You want your money working for you.

Mutual funds are simpler to manage if you have some investment know-how. There are mutual funds for different sectors of the securities market. Pick your sectors and invest. Go for a high rate of return and a reasonable expense ratio with a reputable investment company. As time passes, you will gain more understanding on the right investment mix and risk tolerance for you. Rebalance your mutual fund sector ratio as needed.

As in a hundred-meter race, stalling at the starting point will cost you. Not investing early in life will rob you of compound interest. Take advantage of the magic of compound interest, reinvest, and make the rate of return on compounding principle your friend.

Try to double your base investment within six years by aggressively investing in a mix of sectors. By the time you become a senior citizen, you will be impressed with the growth and appreciation of your investment.

If you have a lump sum of money, invest it soon to get your money working for you. Otherwise, consider dollar cost averaging (regular periodic investment of smaller amounts over time). Dollar cost average contribution is good, but you can also smartly hold on to your savings, Watch the market—and only buy when the market is down. Avoid panic selling during market downturns. Pay attention to the market, particularly any news that affects your holdings. Investments are not a fire-and-forget enterprise; there is always risk and the potential for losing your principal. You will get better outcomes with active interest in your investment management.

Investment rules 7-2 and 1-15 illustrate the power of compound interest. They are the rule of thumb to help with mental calculations for reaching your investment return target. Rule 7-2 is used to find out how long it will take your investment to double. Divide 7-2 with a given fixed rate of return. At a 12 percent rate of return, your base investment value is expected to double in six years, which is 7-2 divided by 12.

Rule 1-15 is used to get insight on the number of years for your investment value to triple. At a 10 percent rate of return, your investment value is expected to triple in eleven and a half years, which is 1-15 divided by 10. Since rates of return go up and down, this should be viewed as a rule of thumb.

Find out your annual maximum IRA contribution limit; if feasible, make the maximum contribution. With a Roth IRA, the taxes are front-loaded, and later gains are nontaxable if you make withdrawals after fifty-nine and half years of age. The Roth IRA works best when you expect your income in retirement to be greater than your income when you are actively working.

Never pass up on your employer's retirement benefit plans. Put your entire retirement nest egg into aggressive investments for the long term. If you have a child, add a 529 college program into your aggressive investment strategy mix. Start it the year each of your kids were born. Your tax-free 529 investment gains are used to pay for eligible college tuition and expenses. Contribute as much as possible to each of your 529 accounts. After eighteen years, your investment could have a significant balance to help send your kids off to college.

Finally, understand the paradox: money is not everything, but money is everything. You may be able to buy the world, but will that make you happy? Learn to live a balanced, fun life that enriches you and the many people you touch. You will not take your wealth to heaven.

Yes, life is full of challenges, but with money, things are easier. Do what you need to do before you do what you want to do. Spend wisely, save, and invest. Use all your bandwidth and operate at the right frequency and wavelength to reach your potential.

Being financially savvy will enhance your chances of becoming economically sufficient—and possibly living a happy life. Those born into substantial wealth or self-made rich individuals enjoy financial freedom that is not common for the public at large. If you are born into humble means, an extravagant and wasteful lifestyle should not be your thing—unless you want to end up being poorer.

CHAPTER 15

CREDIT SCORES

GG says your credit score significantly affects your ability to get loans and build wealth. Lenders use your credit score—creditworthiness, ability to repay, and default probability—to determine your interest rates. An excellent credit score means a cheaper loan, which means you keep more of your money in your pocket.

Unless you do cash-and-carry for everything you purchase, you will likely find yourself in the world of making purchases on credit. You will find yourself entangled in the web of credit score use to determine your loan interest rate and even the products lenders offer you.

Credit scores help lenders establish who is financially responsible and a worthy credit risk. Also, a credit score combined with other personal information can easily be used to tell your character and extrapolate the lifestyle you live. An excellent credit score is a boon. A bad credit score is an albatross that will stifle your financial freedom.

As a young person, you will start off with low credit score due to no credit history. Key elements of credit score include length of credit history; payment history; credit use rate; hard inquiries;

derogatory remarks; and credit mix (credit cards and installment loans such as auto loan, real estate loans, student loans). Negative information like payment delinquency and collections efforts will stay on your record for up to seven years. Your closed credit accounts stay on record for up to ten years.

A perfect credit score is 850, a score achieved by very low number of people. Credit scores above eight hundred are excellent, which puts you in elite status. Credit scores of 750 and higher allow buyers to qualify for better interest rates and product offers. For average and below credit scores, expect higher interest rates. If you have bad credit score, in the lower six hundreds, you will pay cutthroat interest rates or be denied the loan completely.

The best interest rates go to borrowers with excellent credit scores. Excellent credit scores can fetch up to 2 percent cheaper interest rate than for borrowers with lower-than-average credit scores. As credit score declines from excellent to above average to average and lower, the more expensive the loan becomes. Generally, expect about half a percent interest rate differential in descending order from one level to another. While half a percent may appear small, over the life of an installment loan, the total interest rate amount will be significant.

Your goal should be to achieve an excellent credit score, above eight hundred, as soon as possible. Start building your credit history as early as possible. You should try to get your first credit card between eighteen and twenty-two. Retain and keep credit cards open to build your credit. There is negative impact for canceling a credit card. A ten-year average credit age is considered ample. Of course, make 100 percent on-time payments. It is great if your credit use rate is under 30 percent of your available credit balance. It troubles lenders when you have 30 percent or more credit usage rate, which signals you may be financially overextended. A good credit mix speaks to your stability as a borrower. Cultivate habits that nurture excellent or above average credit scores.

To help you monitor and manage your credit records, request the government-authorized free-issue annual credit report at https://www.annualcreditreport.com/index.action. The annual credit report does not include your credit score, but you can subscribe to the three credit bureaus (TransUnion, Equifax, and Experian) for specialized credit products. Websites like Credit Karma, Wallet Hub, and Credit Sesame offer some form of free credit scores regularly.

Check your credit report for accuracy. If you notice discrepancies, submit a dispute and ask for a correction. Any efforts to maintain an excellent credit score is worth the opportunity for cheaper loans. The importance of an excellent credit score cannot be overemphasized.

CHAPTER 16

INSURANCE

As you embark on your life journey, GG says you will need to buy insurance, which is protection from financial risks and losses. You can have insurance coverage for a litany of items and activities. And there are many reasons to have it. You need to have health insurance. You must also address your basic life insurance, homeowner's insurance, and auto insurance needs. They are required elements for wealth management.

Are you confused about how and when to buy a life insurance? Many people are. The probability of young people dying before midlife is low, barring tragic deaths, but have you ever thought you could be the exception? Life insurance premium for young people is fairly cheap. Out of the various life insurance plans, term life insurance appeals to me most. It is the cheapest of all the plans. As a young person, you get more for your buck. Risky lifestyle choices, including cigarette smoking and other risky behaviors, will impact your insurability. Try to avoid a risky lifestyle.

Whole or universal life insurance coverages are also available. From midlife on, life insurance premiums tend to rise steeply, and they become exorbitantly expensive after age seventy. As you get older, insurers are more likely to demand medical examinations to ensure you have no preexisting conditions before issuing a contract.

Try to get term life coverage for about five times your annual income as soon as you can afford the premium. Conduct research and find a reputable insurer with a competitive premium. You should use an annual premium payment rather than a monthly payment. The former allows you to take advantage of a lower overall cost.

Do you need to keep lifelong life insurance? No. When you have adult children and pass midlife, your term life insurance premium will start to increase astronomically. When that occurs, it may be time to lower the coverage amount or allow the policy to expire.

Do not consider life insurance as an investment vehicle. It is a protective blanket for the ones you love. They will depend on it if your untimely death occurs. It is important to always update your designated beneficiaries list. Be sure you have designated beneficiaries to whom your bank accounts and investment accounts will be payable to upon death.

The need for life insurance wanes as your dependents become more established in their own lives. If your kids are financially depending on you past age seventy, you obviously have more problems than life insurance. If you elect to maintain lifelong life insurance, it will cost you. It probably won't be worth it.

Auto insurance is a requirement to legally operate any vehicle on the roads. Full auto insurance coverage is a must when your vehicle is financed. Many people finance new cars for two to six years. The lender holds a lien on the vehicle until the loan is paid off. Lenders require full insurance (comprehensive and collision coverage) to protect their interests. The owner can buy basic liability insurance that meets state requirement when the car is paid off.

Having comprehensive and collision insurance on a new car for up to eight years from date of purchase makes sense. Keeping coverage longer depends on the individual's ability to pay out-of-pocket costs for a total loss. The equation is simpler when the vehicle is a cash purchase. You may elect any combination of years for full insurance coverage (six years is optimal) and liability insurance on your car, or you can buy minimum liability coverage outright. Try to avoid being penny-wise but pound-foolish.

If you are keeping a vehicle for up to eight years, buying the extended maintenance package at the time of the initial purchase is wise. You may not be prepared for out-of-pocket repairs immediately after the manufacturer's original warranty expires. The extended maintenance should give you peace of mind, but you should forgo it if you intend to keep your car for a shorter period.

Insurance providers use age of driver, driving history, vehicle type and value, level of education, and zip code to determine premiums. Always seek discounts (good student, loyalty, and multiple car coverage) when applicable. Also, know the deductible amount for your insurance coverage. Weigh your options between a thousand or two thousand dollars. Choose what you can afford. If you do not ask the insurer for the best deal, they might not offer it to you.

To lower your insurance premiums, aggressively seek discounts from the insurers.

Do your research and buy a reliable vehicle with great re-sale value. A three-or-four-year-old car is about 30–40 percent cheaper than the original MSRP, and it will serve the second owner for up to six more years if it is maintained. You can expect a good service span—up to ten years—if the car you purchase is new and kept up to the manufacturer's maintenance standards.

Within eight or ten years, a vehicle should be in the hands of the second owner—if not the third owner. The vehicle cycle of life continues until it can no longer be of service to anyone. It is then out of commission or salvaged. Older vehicles have higher maintenance costs. They are generally behind in mechanical advances and safety technology. It is your choice when to shift down on your insurance coverage from full to liability and when to sell the vehicle. For better prices and less time at car dealership, shop online. Once you have decided on the type, make, and model, identify dealerships within a hundred miles or so. You will be amazed by their incentives and price differences. To secure ultimate deals, be flexible, particularly with colors and options.

Use the top auto websites (RealCarTips, TrueCar, CarGurus, Kelley Blue Book, Auto Trader, iSeeCars, Edmunds, Carsdirect, Carvana, and CarMax) to see what others have paid for similar cars. You can buy a vehicle at one dealership and service it at a different dealership. When purchasing a vehicle, buy wherever you get the most bang for your buck.

When you buy a used car, it is often sold as is. You may invest in having the car checked out by a good mechanic before you buy it. Beware of the borrowing costs, depreciation costs, and maintenance costs. They can affect your life savings and the wealth you want to build.

Homeowner's insurance is critical part of homeownership. Do not under-insure your home because you risk backbreaking out-of-pocket costs in the event of a total loss. Get an appropriate homeowner's policy that only requires you to pay your chosen deductible following the partial or total loss of your home.

Weeks before you close on a house, get several quotes from different insurance agencies, particularly from the builder's insurer, if available. Do a deep dive on different insurers. Use rating agencies like the A. M. Best, Fitch, Moody's, and Standard & Poor's that assess the major insurance companies' financial strength.

"A" or better rated insurance companies are generally considered financial healthy, which increases the odds that the company will be there when you need them. Pick a company with a proven record and the greatest value for your money. Home insurance coverage includes fire, lightning, wind, and hail, but these are not written in stone. You must review the coverage summary notes to know the scope of your agreement. Earthquakes and floods are typically excluded from homeowner's insurance, but they can be added.

Insurers use proprietary software to look at multiple factors (credit score, neighborhood, real estate market, demographics, age of home, area claim history, fire alarm, home security, pets, number of inhabitants) and calculate your premium. Older homes tend to require more repairs and maintenance, which may translate to higher premiums.

Seek full dwelling and personal property replacement coverage. Always ask the insurance agent to assist you with navigating the process and secure the best discounts that cover total loss with an affordable deductible. Review your quote details, dwelling coverages, other structures, personal property, additional living expenses, personal liability, medical payment, policy deductibles, exclusions, and additional information. Ask for adjustments to the coverage as you desire, strike the right coverage and risk balance, and pick the best coverage and value for you.

Depending on where your home is located, flood insurance may not be critical. It might be good to have. Do some legwork to determine if your home is in a flood zone. You may use the US Federal Emergency Management Agency (FEMA) flood map service center or your city's flood map to gauge your flood risk.

Be cautious. Today's climate unpredictability may be a good enough reason to buy into the national flood insurance program to cover your home and its contents for flood risks that are excluded in basic homeowner's insurance.

Some homeowners buy a home warranty contract to repair or replace big-ticket appliances and electrical, plumbing, heating, and air-conditioning systems. Some people never buy home warranties. They elect to fix or replace their appliances and old systems out of pocket. Make your decision based on your individual financial situation. Remember that hope is not a plan.

While an insurance agent's assistance in evaluating your insurance risks and coverages is invaluable, you must do your own research. Shop around and bundle your insurance policies (life, auto, and home). Insurances quotes can vary significantly between companies. You can get sweeter deals—more than 10 percent discounts—when you bundle your insurance policies.

PART IV

FAMILY

GG's third and final pillar of life is family. Without family, you are like a lone person stranded on an island. Your individual fears and weaknesses will multiply disproportionately. Everybody needs family. You need it too. Family will make a big difference in your life experiences. Family relationships require a lot of work.

As a young man, learning about girlfriends and marriage are worth your time. Your relationships with your family members can bring happiness or feuds. Your love and appreciation for your parents should be second to none. End-of-life discussions should not be a taboo or overlooked.

CHAPTER 17

GIRLFRIENDS

GG says nowhere is elderly guidance more important than in a boy understanding how to deal with his girlfriend. Nowhere is the call of nature more pronounced than a boy liking a girl. It is magnetic.

You may feel a pull toward a girl—even an uncontrollable pull. However, you still have to overcome your inhibitions. You may be shy about expressing your feelings to a girl. You may not be bold enough to say what is on your mind.

The fact that girls often hang around other girls may stymie your courage to go break the ice. Also, your parents may not fully support you focusing on girls at your age. You have quite a hill to climb, but do not be afraid. Like a gentleman, go up to the girl you like. Tell her how you feel about her. That is spunk. Mute your fear of rejection. Do not be afraid of the possible gossip if you try and fail. Everyone who has tried a lot of things has failed at something. Some type of rejection from a girl is scar worn by all mortal men.

Girls share similar limitations and some social norm inhibitions. In general, a good number of girls deliberately act like they have no interest in boys, including you. When it comes to boys, girls are less available, and they are more selective. They can act in a manner that is not easy to catch.

When you like a girl, and she likes you too, your feelings toward each other are not as complicated as you would imagine. Deliberate eye contact is common. After all, the eye is the window to the soul. Puckered-up lips are a giveaway. An approving, soft smile is common. Warm, sensuous body touches are common. Small talk turns to deeper conversations. Your interest in each other will lock in, and she will say, "Meet me by the river."

A girl who is into you might take quick peeks at you. She might blush, fidget around you, or giggle. She might welcome anything that put her in your orbit. She might tolerate your whims and fancies. She might show interest in your personal life. She might be complimentary. She might even shower you with keepsakes.

When you like a girl, and she is not into you, expect polite but cold treatment or a negative verbal rebuff accompanied by hand gestures. Persevere a bit if you really like the girl. Do not give in at the first no. Try to show her you care about her. Woo her. Try, try, and try again. If she claims to always be busy, you are not a priority for her. If her rejection persists or increases, leave her alone and move on. Many girls have rejected the boys who liked them, but later in life, they wished their actions were different.

Girls like handsome boys. Boys with good physical features will enjoy more attention from girls. An easy smile goes a long way with girls. Ease of conversation and establishing rapport and common interests with a girl will do wonders.

Boys who are social butterflies are good catches for girls. Being book smart is a plus. Street smarts are attractive to some girls—but not all of them. Athletic prowess can get guys to the center stage. Making people laugh is a likeable quality. Being humble and being an underdog will earn a boy a darling reputation. Your hair and clothes make a statement about who you are and who you want to be. Oral hygiene, body hygiene, and clean clothing matter. Girls tend to gravitate to boys who appear to have bright futures ahead of them. They want guys who care about their feelings and guys who they feel safe around. Lies can break friendships. Being honest will lighten the burden of trying to remember your previous lies. Alcohol and substance abuse are detrimental to a good life and good relationships. Being controlling shows insecurity, which will damage your relationship with a girl. Trust her until you are proven wrong. Infidelity will kill your relationship faster than almost any other problem. Girls like trustworthy guys with spunk and a sense of purpose. Be that guy.

Do not read a girl's cues with one eye open and the other closed because you may be looking at a mirage. Deciphering a girl's cues can be more challenging than untangling a fish net and a Rubik's cube at the same time. Just do your best.

What if you have found a girl you like, but you are not sure if she is truly the right one? Look a little deeper to see if she has rage inside or will explode like a volcano. What she does and says when she is angry reveals her true self. Her internal anger could be like poison. Just like a wildfire or a war, it could start small and then escalate and cause massive destruction. If she becomes your girlfriend, you too will bear her wrath. Emotions do not respect boundaries.

Is she a drama queen? Does she see only one sentence in a conversation, which creates a downward spiral? Watch out for sins of omission. Are there any crazy antics? Like with rats, when there is one, there are many more.

Does she nag? Does she turn little things into crises? Is she someone who will not spare you the details if she knocked down all ten pins while bowling? Does she twist herself into a pretzel for no reason? Is she defensive? Does her behavior keep you on the razor's edge? These habits will always resurface; it is just matter of when.

Can you tell her breaking point? Look under the hood to see how things work. Check for crosscurrents and underwater currents. Is danger—like sharks or marine predators—lurking? Can you live with that? Will she forgive and forget? Does she want peace? Is she vengeful? Is she the silent type? Silence is not inactivity. Does she apologize readily because she values your relationship more than sticking to her guns to prove she is right? If she pulls you together—and not apart, it must not be lost on you.

A good number of girls take pleasure in shopping. Do not try to figure that out. If you do, you will have a headache. Look out for ungratefulness. Everyone likes to be respected and appreciated. Do not neglect or forget her attitude. Do not assume you know what she is thinking. Be conscious of her emotions. Judging is a task for the impartial.

If your reputation matters, gallivanting from one girl to another is recipe for disaster. Be judicious and discerning when choosing a girlfriend.

Think about a lifelong partner when you look for a girlfriend because she could end up being your wife. Do not abuse her or take advantage of her; she could be the future mother of your children, your bloodline, and your legacy. Her voice should be soothing to your soul. She should care about your feelings and happiness and not be needy.

Love is two-way street, and it must be nurtured. There is no guarantee that your first girlfriend will be your wife, but sticking to similar types of girls will allow people to offer advice about your relationship choices. Let your parents meet your girlfriend. Showing her off to your family will do more good than bad. If you listen to your family's input, you will not regret one of life's biggest decisions: marriage.

Your relationship with her should be a litmus test for your commitment. Should you marry or not marry her? Take a pass if you harbor serious doubts about the relationship. It is best to close the stable door when the horse is inside and not after the horse has left the barn. Once you are married, all bets are off. There is rarely enough time to raise a red flag in front of a raging bull.

Before you pull the plug, make sure you are not undervaluing the things you have at the cost of what you wish you have. Appreciate your girlfriend's compassion, patience, and other virtues. Do not demand perfection; be happy with excellence. If you have problem with everything, you are probably the problem. Have a reality check about your expectations.

Is she the one? Think about how much you appreciate her and miss her. When you are with her, is she more interested in your time than your things? Avoid high-maintenance relationships. Who wants someone who drains them? When you are with her, watch for kids riding bicycles on the street when a car is coming— and note her concerns and reactions. Is she caring, empathetic, or helpful? Did her reaction capture your fancy? You may have to move on if the chemistry is off, or you might end up loving her more without knowing why. Forgive yourself. People love or hate for infinite reasons. Opposites attract. It could simply be an accident of history.

Fall in love with her whole person and not just her skin-deep beauty. Do not be over your head in love and miss seeing the forest for the trees. Keep the hot side hot and the cool side cool. Do not run off to measure the curtains when you still have to build the house. The curtains might not match the rug. What a haphazard arrangement. A solid relationship requires deliberate effort.

Doing your due diligence will prevent you from being a raffle ticket with higher odds of losing than winning. The girl you choose should have the personality, smarts, talents, and looks you yearn for.

When you pick the right girl, be ready to express your love verbally and physically every day. Be the real you with no holds barred. Give her hints about all the chapters of your life rather than keeping them unpublished. If she reciprocates, be all ears, show her you are into her, and speak up only as required. Remember to exercise the gavel in your hand. Your new lover should not expect you to be a rubber stamp for her whims and caprices. Girls want guys who act like real men. You must be assertive and carry your load.

Behind many successful men are the great women who love and support them. Are you prepared to have your current girlfriend be one of your handful of lifelong friends and confidantes? Over time, your valued friends will shrink to just a few, and your wife-to-be ought to make the list.

Marry a girl who completes you—and not one who will finish you. The former will add to your strengths and bridge your weaknesses. The latter will undermine you, make your days worse, and add chaos or misery. Are you marrying someone who completes you or finishes you? Many girls will kill for you, but only a few—a loving wife, your mother, and maybe your sister—will die for you.

The wife you pick will influence your life journey more than you can ever imagine. Be careful about who you truly want and who you can truly live with. What are you willing to give up? Separate the wheat from the chaff. The right choice is a treasure, but a mistake can set the stage for lot of pain and unhappiness down the road.

Have a commonsense approach to life. When the desirable is not available, the available becomes the desirable. Focus more on the character of the girl than her appearance. The way you relate to each other in good and bad times is important. In bad times, you will be tested and stretched to the limit. A good wife will weather the storm with you.

Look for a partner with complementary traits. No man or woman is an island. To make your team stronger, welcome her independent voice. She will help you find your way, learn, and grow. Be leery of controversial personalities—unless you want to spin in place and generate friction and heat until you exhaust yourself and go kaput.

Life is a process. Make room for acquired tastes along the way. Oceanfront stores should be prepared for hurricane-induced waves. Does your girlfriend pass the test? She should stand out as a unique tree in a forest. Can you see her in the crowd of girls out there?

Love can be blind. When you love her, race, age, weight, and height are valueless stats. When her guard is down, how does she talk about people, particularly folks she does not approve of? How does she treat people with lower economic status? Watch out for quick-to-angered and grudge-bearing women. They can be a nightmare.

Does she often drink one too many? If yes, buckle up because there are more problems where that came from. Being jealous and controlling are sins you could be reluctant to talk about. Jealousy destroys trust. Being controlling can suck the oxygen out of a relationship. Why marry someone who is jealous and controlling?

What are her thoughts about your relationships with your mother and your siblings? Does she see your tight bond with your family as a threat? Her relationships with her own siblings matter too. Watch out for red flags.

Watch out for what is not being said. What is not being said can reveal more about the person than what is being said. Be vigilant for unique facial, hand, and leg reactions and signature movements; they could be part of her story.

Do not expect to find the perfect person. If you are comparable in many ways, ask yourself if you are happy with what you have seen thus far. If all is going well, address the common relationship problems. Money is the root of many problems. Poor financial arrangements can doom a marriage. Consider setting up individual and joint accounts. Determine what financial arrangements suit your relationship. Hashing out the rules of the game early on will save you tons of headaches later, and it will help with smoother operations at home.

A beautiful marriage starts with selecting the right girlfriend and picking the right wife.

Do your homework long before you ask her to marry you. Do you really know her? Would you be thrilled to be in the same room with her forever? If you are excited about that possibility, keep the ball rolling. Do you have reservations about her being the mother of your kids? Your kids will pick up her traits too. Does she lie about little things and big things? Would you entrust your life in her hands? If you lose your trust in her, you lose her worth. Building a relationship on violated trust is like building a house on shifting sands.

Does she always have to be right? If she is, people will talk about her superiority complex. She will not be able to bring out the best in others, and her actions will turn off other people. That's not funny. Getting married to her would be like riding a speeding train off a cliff. In a good relationship or marriage, being right is not the most important thing; being accommodating, strong, and tender is more important.

Are you the type of man who easily waves off the enormous demands of running a home? What about doing chores, the minutia of day-to-day living, and pinching pennies to keep a happy home? She needs supportive attention. Talk about this to get a better idea about the role your wife-to-be wants you to play.

Many mothers choose to be homemakers and handle the immense tasks of managing the welfare, good order, and discipline of the household. Make it clear that you appreciate your homemaking wife's contributions as much as if you were in a two-income household. Working inside or outside the home is equally important.

It is great if your wife to be works outside the home. Two-income household tend to have more discretionary funds at their disposal. What if she wants to make her own money and not depend on you for everything? Depending on your stage in life, an outside job could be suitable. This might change as your family evolves. Either way, discuss these scenarios and support her preference to be homemaker or not. You might even be a stay-at-home husband.

Be honest with her in all your discussions. Do unto others as you would want done unto you. If you have anything you could never give up, speak up, set limits, and establish boundaries. What is good for the goose is good for the gander. Your wife-to-be is assessing you too. Just as you look into a mirror, the mirror looks back at you.

Be open to finding love in unusual places. Do not be shy about expressing your love for the girl you care for. Do not let physical attraction decide everything—and be prepared to accept rejection.

When you find the love of your life, you will know. Your plans will complement each other. Your thoughts will be occupied by the things you will do to make each other happy. That feeling will be mutual and reciprocal. Your true friends and close family members will see it for what it is, and they will approve.

You will know you have picked the right lifelong mate if you are more in sync than apart. Propose to her if she is the right one. When she says, "Yes," your fate is sealed. The hard work of having a beautiful marriage begins.

CHAPTER 18

MARRIAGE

Who says marriage is easy? GG says that marriage is the strongest relationship you can have—and it must not be taken for granted. It is more than doing business with a handshake. If you piss on your marriage, you will quickly discover that you have violated the contract. A broken marriage is akin to a broken covenant—people get hurt.

When you commit to marriage, you commit to the ultimate lifelong partnership. You gain new titles: husband and wife, possibly parents, maybe grandparents. You and your wife will share and manage most of your lives together. When you are best friends, your marriage will be sweeter than sweet.

In your marriage, it is imperative to have a good start. Begin as good friends, graduate to being boyfriend and girlfriend, and then make her your queen and dignified wife.

Most couples lock into matrimony in the heat of passion. A good number of marriages, for one reason or another, end in divorce. No one prays to be one of those statistics, but that is life. You do not want to have firsthand experience with the sting of divorce. Many divorcees experience lifelong agony as a result of the experiment. Avoid the divorce experience.

Marry for life. Enjoy the honeymoon phase, nurture the guard-down reality phase, and accept your fate. Marriage until death should be your goal.

Marriage should be a lifelong commitment where husband and wife routinely try to outdo each other in making each other happy. A flash-in-the-pan romance has no chance, and a slow-burning romance leaves plenty of room for extramarital affairs. If you are with the love of your life—the best of them all—why would you care about the rest of the girls out there?

If you are not ready for marriage, stay away. If you want and need it, be present in it and give it all your love. Tame your libido, never allow it to overtake your common sense, and refuse to commit adultery.

A great marriage demands total alignment. What do you need to do to succeed in your marriage? Tie your decisions to the necessary actions. If you put your money where your mouth is, you will succeed. True love is the inevitable glue in a successful marriage. Love runs in the background. It does not cast shadows or suffocate. It is warm, approving, and supportive.

A touch of kindness on physical and emotional levels is required in love. Enabling your partner to be their best self is required in love. Patience in quiet mode—devoid of flippancy or jitters—is showing respect and love.

A sign of love falling apart is talking over each other. That masks the real problem and allows the problem to fester and grow. The problem feeds on itself and self-destructs.

Abuse of any type takes away from love, and it will put you in the club no real man wants to join: the spouse abuser's club.

Leverage special moments to amplify your love for your wife. Love requires you to give each other a little more than you take from the other person. Do not give one and take one or two. It is *b*etter to give three and take one. The key is to appreciate each other. Her love for you and your love for her should be a two-way street—give and take, equal and opposite, but contextually more. True love is hard to define. If you love each other for better and for worse, when your looks have faded and the romance has fizzled, your unique bond and love for each other will enable you to survive and make each other feel like the next day is going to be better.

Your marriage can be as beautiful as you want it to be, but it is going to take dedication and hard work. It will take a lot of high-wire balancing acts to keep the beautiful flower blooming and your home looking sweet. Seeing your partner's approving smile every day will make all the effort worthwhile.

Lying kills a marriage. Be straight and truthful because bad news does not get better with age. The unvarnished truth does not evolve. If you cannot take the heat, get out of the kitchen. Talk daily and compromise on disagreeable issues.

Your duty is to make your wife happy. Treat your wife as the chosen one. Ask what makes her glow. Do it. In public, uplift her. At home, make her happy. Behind closed doors, her satisfaction must precede yours. Lessons from the *Kama Sutra* may be helpful. When your wife makes the first touch, reciprocate. Do you know what sends her over the moon? How much time do you spend with your wife in a day? Friendship and building closeness require time.

Every day, tell and show your wife you love her. When you are at home, be at home. In public, put your wife on a pedestal. Never stop fanning the love flame between you and your wife. Otherwise, the love will go cold. A good marriage must be serviced and maintained.

Your number one job as a husband is to take care of your wife and kids, fend for them, and protect them. Do not suffocate them with obsessive attention. Avoid jealousy and possessiveness.

All members of a family are different, and what they see depends on where they stand. Everybody having a vote can make diversity a strength. Nurture the differences because when everyone is thinking alike, no one is thinking. Leverage opposing perspectives to make your marriage and home stronger than ever.

Maintaining a healthy relationship with your wife should be a top priority. Your relationship with your parents and siblings should be a distant second place. Your relationship with others must not be at the expense of your relationship with your wife. Peace and charity begin at home, but they should not end there.

If you are so blessed, you and your wife will procreate within thirty-six months of marriage. Remember that man proposes—and God disposes.

During pregnancy and after the birth of your first child, you and your wife will be introduced to the real stress of a marriage. Your wife may be less independent, experience mood swings and energy fluctuations, crave your affection and reassurance, and be afraid of the uncertainty of motherhood. Be sensitive and caring to the changes your wife is going through. Provide a shoulder for her to lean on. Be there for her. Your voice and presence should be soothing to your wife. If you have fears, share them with her—and promise that you are together in this. That is when you need to earn your badge of honor as the man and the husband she married.

By about thirty-three years of age, you should have had your first kid. If you want a second kid—or whatever number of kids you elect to have—try to be done by midlife. Two or three kids are ample unless you think your mission is to populate the world and spend your life worrying about what your kids are up to. Are three kids not enough to replace you and your wife plus one more?

Having more kids means carrying more parental loads during your life journey. While your kids may turn out to be the pride and joy of your life, the responsibility of raising them is no joke.

There are no guarantees that all your kids will see things as you see them. It is not selfish to plan to have fewer kids and have more time and resources to lend a hand to others who are less privileged.

Having kids around thirty allows you to still be healthy enough to play and run around with your kids before they start outsprinting you. That could happen eventually, but do not let it happen before your kids are teenagers.

It is amusing to hear your kids bragging about outsprinting you, their daddy, and the fun is at your expense. Of course, you can do a lot of other fun activities with them. Try fishing, sporting events, or entertaining shows. Find family time to nourish your bond. Enjoy the moment while you can. When your kids grow up, they might not want to hang out with their old man.

Much older parents have physical limitations and excuses for not playing and wrestling with their teenage boys. Do you want to be an old dad?

The timing of when you take on the responsibility of marriage and having kids is important. You can take care of your family better when you take home a handsome paycheck. It is good for the man of the house to still be in the workforce and at his peak earning power when his kids are teenagers. You do not need to have a lot of money, but you need to have enough to manage. Getting kids' their first cars and sending them off to college can be fulfilling. Everything depends on the situation. Do the math and find your own timing.

Accept your kids as they are. Do not compare your kids if you do not want to breed contentious rivalries and hatred among them. Siblings often bear grudges against the perceived favorite child because they fail to see their parents cheering for the good plays of each sibling and admonishing bad behaviors equally. When your parents call you out for what you have failed at, listen, pay attention, and do things right. Don't hate your siblings or breed divisiveness in your family.

Teach your kids with your examples. Illustrate the lessons and apply them. Stay even-keeled. Let your actions and demeanor show that you always have situations under control. In raising kids, a high ethical standard is priceless. Do not fall for kids' control gimmicks. Don't let the kids play the parents. Have a game plan to avoid kids pitching Mom against Dad. Let Mom respond first and have daddy be quiet. If necessary, Daddy can reaffirm Mom's position. Also, Mom backs Daddy if the shoe is on the other foot. That is a winning strategy.

Your kids will learn using the crawl-walk-run approach. Recognize and praise their slightest progress. If you tell your kids they are the best, they will believe you. Mom and Dad's approval means the world to them. It builds their confidence and courage to engage in the world and seek and gain the approval of their peers.

Your support—or lack of it—will impact who your kids turn out to be in later years. Children thrive when they have level-headed parents who support them come rain or shine. Absent parents are like a cog in the wheel of their kids' growth and success. Kids need parents to be present in their lives.

Expect to be a grandparent at around sixty years old. Ensure your grandkids are not left out. Spend quality time doing things with them. Funny memories of these activities will mean more to you and to them as your ages creep up. Quality time with your grandkids will be among their favorite times. Treasure them.

If your wife offends you, be very forgiving. Really forgive and forget. When there are conflicts, learn to forgive before the problem grows. Do not allow your anger to brew, simmer, or age like wine. The longer anger ferments, the more the bitterness will entrench in your mind. It can be revived as easily as a smoldering ember. It can be like cut grass that grows again later. A stitch in time saves nine.

When you and your wife disagree or argue, you should bury the hatchet before you both fall asleep. Your anger should not last more than twenty-four hours. If you have frequent or longer quarrels, you will make everyone in your household feel like they are drinking from a poisoned water fountain. You do not want to create a bad family dynamic. The sooner you and your wife talk and resolve the disagreement and apologize to each other, the better.

As human beings, imperfect in nature, there will be times when discussions turn into heated arguments. Couples in beautiful marriages tend to have circuit breakers or escape hatches to defuse hot-air situations before they combust. Agree with wife on your resolution approach. Someone—you or her—needs to be the peacemaker. If an argument occurs, walk away first. If your wife walks away first, do not follow her. Give her space to cool off. Does the argument offend your pride?

One of the best approaches is to stop talking once you sense a problem in your discussion. When you are explaining, you are losing. Most of the time, the listener has their mind made up, and your explanation is adding salt to the injury and prolonging the agony.

Quickly end the back-and-forth exchange. Give yourself a time-out. You are not supposed to win a verbal feud with your wife unless you plan to be a miserable husband. Walk away from the situation. Go get some fresh air into your lungs.

After a few hours of cool-down time, go back to your wife and apologize for allowing yourself to get carried away in vigorously stating your viewpoint. Real men admit their mistakes.

Figure out the best time to engage with your wife on hot-button issues. This time, make a deliberate effort to compromise and solve the problem.

Your wife has her own mind, and she wants to do certain things her own way. Learn to watch and listen without giving your opinion. Sometimes all she wants is your affirmation. Sometimes, all she wants is your silent approval. Show her you heard and understood what she was saying. Give her recognition. If you must say something, encourage and support her.

If you want an argument-free home and a happy wife, be sensitive, appreciative, and respectful. To give her a break, you should diligently do what she wants you to do.

If your kids intercede in an out-of-control argument between you and your wife, that is an indication of trouble in your household. You are likely not being a good example for your kids. Spouses fighting in front of their kids leaves bad memories that they wish they could forget.

No proud father would bask in the sun and rejoice about the injuries he has inflicted upon his family. He could lose his wife, his kids, and the good name of his family.

Out-of-control arguments must be avoided at all costs. It is a losing game that you need not play. It is OK not to feel OK. Seek help if you feel overwhelmed. A closed mouth does not get fed. For sticky points you cannot resolve, seek advice from a family member who you respect. Hold off on seeking an outsiders' counsel unless the problem persists.

With open minds, consideration for each other, and the desire to sincerely find a solution, you and your wife can adjust your initial positions and reach a common ground for the good of your family. Battling differences in opinion for consensus is democracy in action.

Be a gentleman. Create argument-free conditions in your home. Be faithful. Be respectful. Be kind. Show compassion. Be caring. Be chivalrous. Every day, give your wife more than a peck of kiss. Touch her and hug her to reaffirm your commitment to your marriage vows. Treat your wife like the queen she is, and she will make you the king of the castle. Do everything possible to keep your marriage together.

In a marriage, the details you see depend upon your level of attention. Learn a lot about your wife. Accept that your wife—like other women—is very powerful. Read biographies of notable women and romance books. Find insights into their unique powers, challenges, feelings, and desires. The more you know, the more you can relate, empathize, and love.

Love is strange. It can wind you up, undress you, screw you, and leave you on your own.

Understand the landscape of a marriage. While you may see sex and love as two different things, many women see them as one and the same. Many women want their feelings to be the first layer of the act, which is contrary to men's desire for the act to precede any real relationship.

Understand the power of money. Many women get married for economic reasons rather than love. If you have money, a lot of women will find you attractive, which implies that you will be at a higher risk for flirtation. What are your control measures?

Fighting over money is one of the most common sins in a marriage. One person is always the spender, and the other is the saver. Spend time discussing how to manage the family's finances way before saying I do. Accept your initial agreement as the starting point of a work-in-progress project.

A marriage cannot be drilled down to a simple formula. Marriage is a risky business. It will take devotion for your marriage to thrive. Unfortunately, one of you can send the union to divorce court. A good marriage requires hard work and two people who want their marriage to work. A marriage is not just between the husband and wife. To some extent, a marriage reaches deep into the extended family. There are some responsibilities.

If you or your wife is derelict about your responsibilities, the other is powerless in changing that decision. The person you love is supposed to love you back, but it does not always work out that way.

A good marriage is a reciprocal relationship. Choose a partner who fits the bill. A successful marriage is desired by most men and women. Good marriages are made. Excellence is the goal—not perfection. Love is an important ingredient for a healthy marriage, but it is not how much you love your wife; it is how much you can put up with her. Your wife shares the team captainship with you. Respect her as you would respect your boss and your mother combined.

Your wife is not a minister without a portfolio. Share your goals and targets in life with her. You will discover that she is your greatest cheerleader. If the shoes were on the other feet, she knows you would cover her six. Enjoy and suffer together rather than alone.

Marriage requires a ton of grace and wisdom. Marriage is not always romantic. The movies play, and the music ends. Laughter and tears follow. A fresh scene emerges with a new perspective. Things often change in a marriage.

A flourishing marriage includes no physical abuse. No matter the circumstances, never beat your wife. Contain your foul mouth and no touching. Never blame anger—and keep your hands to yourself. Would you like another man to beat your mother or sister? How would you like a stronger guy beating you up? Wife beating is a badge of infamy that you do not want to wear. Physical abuse is a no-no and a crime.

Marriage is not a passive vocation. You get a wife in a marriage. A wife gives you companionship that no one else can give. It is a partnership that works together naked and not ashamed. It will change your existing friendships. Think and talk about those realities and adapt.

A good marriage is a relationship between best friends. Best friends are hard to find and even harder to keep. Some aspects of your life will be a joint venture, and some will remain a private enterprise. Marriage is not meant to strip your individuality; it should make the goodness in you and your wife better.

It takes a lot for a marriage to get through a day. Since you live in a twenty-four-seven world and share emotions, leave your vulnerabilities open to each other's peering eyes. Accept them and leverage your union. She knows your strengths, weaknesses, tendencies, and blind spots. No couple is perfect, and no couple has it all together. Learn to always negotiate for peace.

If the first person you tell good news to is not your wife, something is wrong. If your communication resembles a catfight, you are in trouble. If silence is the mode of communication in your household, your marriage is on its way to freezing to death. Communication is oxygen. When your marriage is on the rocks, it is suffocating.

You may need a communication drill. Practice respectful communication. Say only how you feel using "I." Whenever "you" is the subject, your partner's defensive guard will be on high alert, which distracts from good communication. Don't read between the lines. In marriage, assumptions can be dangerous. If you suspect, ask. If you do not know, say so. You are responsible to say what you mean.

Do not chase your wife or stand your ground. Find a way for her to win some while you win some too. Save your pride. Do not use your wife for cheap laughs. Never abandon your wife or kids. Leaving your wife is cowardice. The broken hearts are the ones you ought to protect and provide for.

Your wife deserves a husband and not a man who acts like a child. She wants a partner—not a project. You got married because you felt you were both adults, but there will be occasions that make you doubt whether you know each other well enough. The stress of marriage can make you and your wife think the other one is acting like a child. Would it have been better if you and your wife had gone through each other's responsibilities and expectations prior to saying I do? That rarely happens. No wonder there is confusion in many young couples' expectations. You may be surprised to know how frequently the following scenario plays out:

> Wife: Why do you work all the time and have no time for us? Why are you home all the time? Go make some money like a real man. You are home all day doing nothing. At least clean up after yourself.

> Husband: I am not your child. You do not tell me what to do.

> Wife: Whatever.

If wife ends her utterances with "whatever," more trouble is headed your way. If she gives you the silent treatment, you definitely will have more trouble in the future.

> Husband: Where is all the money? Why are you always on the phone? Who are you talking to?

> Wife: You are not my daddy.

If she brought it up, it bothers her. Look for a sneering look, a high-pitched tone, or tears. That scenario is just a tip of the iceberg of the crazy conversations that occur in a normal married home. There are moments you cannot script.

A marriage needs maintenance. Both of you must carry the water to prevent it from spilling.

Take a daily bath to stay recharged twenty-four-seven. You will need it to stay sane and keep a happy wife, happy kids, and happy father. Figure out how to make things right in your home. Rethink your work life, strike a balance, and try to find the sweet spot.

Just as you figured out how to listen to your mother as a mama's boy, figure out how to listen to your wife as your soul mate. Just as you figured out how to absorb scolding from your mother and boss at work, figure out with your wife what makes for smooth sailing at home.

The man of the house designation is not determined by salary, and the woman of the house is not determined by managing home affairs. Traditionally, the husband ensures food is on the table and bills are paid. He is the breadwinner, and the wife runs the home front. At home, neither of you is confused about who the real captain is: The wife. Mama. The kids love Mama more. Those are unwritten rules.

In the division of labor, strategically pitch parenting and career responsibilities to each other. The success or failure of your marriage relates to your respect for the division of labor. Respect your wife as much as or more than you respect your boss and your icons. She plays a role that no one else can play. Admire your wife because she has a big impact on you and wields influence on your life story.

Do not think you are more valuable than your spouse. Both of you have equal authority in parenthood. As equal partners, neither of you should dictate what the other does for a career.

Know what is good for a team marriage. Carry your cross, keep your end of the bargain, appreciate the art of marriage, and respect each other's role.

Marriage's rewards include physical and emotional comfort and laughter and tears. Your offspring to keep the family tree alive and going. Do not spare the rod and spoil the child. Have principles and keep to them. Teach your kids responsibilities, hold them accountable, and always love them.

Another phenomenal benefit of being married with kids is becoming an overnight expert about everything. Yes, everything. You can go from small talk to matters of the day by using your kids as the stepping-off point to your story. You will be accepted. You will draw approving laughter because they can relate. This works best when you read the room.

A beautiful marriage is a blessing. A beautiful marriage demands disciplined care for your wife. A happy wife makes a happy home. Your household will grow like the biblical mustard seed when you have a happy home. Your wife will be your partner like no other. You will have the reinforcing strength of her company. She will make you a better person than you would be alone. You cannot do better by yourself. Nothing is as invigorating as knowing you are returning home to be welcomed by your caring, loving wife and happy kids.

Acknowledge all your wife does as a supermom for your kids. Do things for yourself. Wash your clothes and pick up after yourself. Help with chores. Get hints from your wife about the areas she wants and needs you to work on.

Do not assume anything. Do not overthink or underthink things. See what your wife wants done on an unfinished project before you run off to finish it. The important thing is not that you did something; it is that you did what she wanted you to do.

Always express your gratitude for the meals your wife prepares for your family. Every now and then, get her gifts to show appreciation for all she does for your household.

Whether your wife works and earns her own money or not, budget for your wife's upkeep. Never forget her routine salon hairdo, pedicure, and manicure. Give your wife pocket money regularly. No matter how small it is, it makes a statement that you have a vested interest in her.

Your wife plays an intermediary role between you and your kids. Sometimes, she will act as their mouthpiece. Welcome her role and empower her by supporting her decisions and commitments with the kids.

A good husband makes a good wife. A good wife makes a good home. Your home is your castle. Other than your life, the last thing you would want to lose is your home. A good husband will do anything to defend his wife and kids.

CHAPTER 19

APPRECIATE YOUR PARENTS

GG says it matters more to give your parents flowers while they are still here than to place flowers on their graves. Appreciate your parents now. Do not wait until tomorrow.

Respect your parents. Never call them by their first names; they are not your classmates. You may call your mother Mama, Mom, Mommy, or any exclusive moniker befitting her special role in your life. You may call your father Papa, Pop, Dad, Daddy, or any other special name. Take pride in the names you call your parents. The names must recognize their unique relationship with you. When your parents hear you say their names, they should be proud and be reminded of your life journey together.

Complaining and blaming your parents for where you are in life is misplaced energy that does no good. Instead, empathize with your parents' story. Your parents will be happier knowing you appreciate them not minding their blemishes and have accepted them as is.

Accept the phase of your parents programming you is done. Good or bad, they have programmed you in the best way they knew how. Accept that reprograming yourself is your job;

hardware renovation, innovation, and software updates are your responsibilities. With the umbrella (genes) that your parents handed off to you, when it rains, you should be OK. In a hurricane, you will be drenched. If you want more than what was passed down to you, add your own wet-weather parka. Find excellence by hard work and become the best you can be. Your parents will take pride in you for reinventing yourself and being on top of your game.

When your vision extends to helping others change their lives for the better, it will give your parents joy. You will gain inner joy when you commit 5 percent or more of your earnings to helping others.

When you enjoy seeing your siblings happy about the things you do for them, and you are the light in the room and get the family laughing, your parents will smile from ear to ear. It feels good to see people smiling and know you are responsible for that.

Getting along with your siblings will be comforting to your parents. Encourage and motivate each other to become your best self. It reassures your parents that their family tree will not be hollowed out by family feuds.

Your parents will adore seeing you laying a foundation for others to follow. Foster team spirit. Enable your siblings to embrace what a man has done, another man can do even better. Teach them the importance of knowing when to stand and fight back and when to run and hide.

No one stays on top forever. You will wax and wane and reach your apex and ebb. Your parents are all too familiar with that situation. Not too many things will appease your parents like helping your siblings pick up the mantle, build upon your success, and be better and greater. You will help them succeed without suffering because you have already suffered for them. Make a path for them and keep it open. Conditions will never be perfect for showing that you love and appreciate your parents.

Family potlucks can make your parents proud. Usually, each person thinks their dish is the best. Be diplomatic in complimenting or criticizing a dish because you may offend someone. Mama wants no bickering. A word or two to the wise is enough. Your parents will cherish the family get-together.

What you say, how you say it, and when you say it can make your siblings smile. Your words are flowers, and your sentences are a bouquet. Your words matter. Each word matters. The beauty of your bouquet depends on the types of flowers and the way they are arranged.

Say good things to make your siblings smile. You will feel better when they are laughing. You will warm your parents' hearts.

One of the best ways to bond with your siblings is showing you care, which is a lot more important than giving material things. Empathy is priceless. Your parents want to see strong bonds among their kids. If your parents love you for always being empathetic, never betray their trust.

An open mind and a welcoming attitude are great starting points for dealing with siblings. Pay attention to the things in front of you—especially your siblings, and never overlook the things on the side. They all want to be recognized and respected.

Change your mind if you hear enlightening messages from any of your siblings. Only a dead person cannot change their mind.

Because time and tide wait for nobody, be spontaneous and responsive in your actions. Your parents will swear by you when they trust your hands are on the steering wheel when it counts. Be as good a follower as you are a leader.

Appreciate your parents, particularly your mother. Most mothers give their kids all they have, and they will even go hungry. Mothers are superhuman. All men should know that and respect that with their actions.

Most mothers are the directors of home affairs or homemakers. A good number of mothers work outside the home to bring home the bacon. Many are the main breadwinners. From dawn to dusk, many mothers are taking care of their families.

Mothers' days are often filled with chores, which would exhaust the strongest men and bring them to their knees in a few days. Late to bed and early to rise represents most mothers. Mothers put their kids to bed and tuck them in at night. Mothers wake up early and get their kids ready for school. Mothers plan the day's meals and ensure their families are fed.

For whatever reason, the cleanliness and orderliness of the house rest on mothers' shoulders. The decoration and comfort of the house depend on the mothers' choices. Keeping kids' appointments and taking them to extracurricular activities are responsibilities that mothers graciously take.

When Mama is happy, the house is happy. Mama is the house cheerleader. Daddy leans on Mama for emotional support, fresh ideas, advice, constructive feedback, and making decisions. The kids run to Mama for almost everything because Mama cares.

Mama does everything within her power to give her kids an abundance of love and as many material things as she can afford. Mama's unconditional love for her family is priceless. She picks out the kids' clothes—and sometimes her husband's clothes. She takes care of the kids and her husband when they are sick.

Mama is the last person on her priority list. By the end of the day, many mothers are spent. Mothers are incredible givers and natural leaders.

Your mother needs a helping hand too. Find ways to help and give your mom a break. Do what Mama asks the first time she gives an order. When she says get up, you should get up. When she tells you to brush your teeth or take shower, do it right away. When she asks you to come to eat, do so and clean up after yourself. When she asks you to do your chores, jump up and get them done. Those little gestures will go a long way in helping her manage the hectic job of running the home and will make her day a bit less daunting.

Eat out for special occasions and special memories. Learn how to cook your favorite foods. Cook foods for your family. Mama will not be there forever. You can pass down family recipes to your own kids. Learn how to cook and help out as required. Your parents will be delighted to see their kids learning secret family recipes.

Be a handyman around the house. Men who do minor home repairs without freaking out when things break at home earn their mothers' respect. You are only respected for what you finished and not what you started.

Get a toolbox and a starter tool set. Buy pliers, wrenches, vise grips, screwdrivers, hammers, measuring tapes, levels, and hand saws. To learn how to fix stuff, make Google and YouTube your friends. The more you fix stuff, the better you get—but leave the electrical repairs to the professionals.

Today's economic conditions have forced more families to become two-income units. In one-income families, the man is usually the breadwinner, and the wife is usually the homemaker. As the cost of living gets higher and higher, it is no longer easy for an average husband to make enough to comfortably sustain the family. Supermom to the rescue! Imagine what single mothers go through to take care of you. They work outside the home and still manage the home. Oh, sweet mothers, thank you for all you do.

When Mom says she will do her best to get you something, believe her. If she did not come through, understand that circumstances beyond her control may have overtaken the promise. Your mom feels bad about breaking her promise, and she might not have conveyed her situation in a manner that soothed your disappointment. That may be the right moment to turn around the situation. Tell her you understand and still love her for being your mother and bringing you into this world. You will make her day because everyone loves to be appreciated. When you are away, call your parents, particularly your mom. Frequently check in with them. It is important that your parents know you are OK. Calling them should give the peace of mind that they are fine too.

If you get good news while you are away, get it reported in your local news outlet. Doing so is not for your benefit; it is for your parents. Your parents will take pride in your success and share the news with your community. Doing so tells your parents you care and love them.

No matter how small your gifts to your parents are, they value them. The thought means more than the dollar value of the gift. To them, it means recognition and appreciation for the hard job of bringing you into the world and raising you to be a contributing citizen of the world. It gives them immeasurable joy and an immeasurable sense of accomplishment. If you want to multiply their happiness, find reasons to shower them with sentimental gifts.

Give your parents a grandkid before you turn thirty or soon thereafter. The longer you hold off, the longer the runway is for their flight to becoming Grandma and Grandpa. Your parents want to have grandkids around, and they want to spoil them. Since grandparents tend to give grandkids more freedom, the kids often come back happier. That is nature's role in the cycle of life.

Be nice to your parents when they bring up conversations about getting married and having children. Their concern is out of love. It is fulfilling for them to know you are carrying on the dynasty and watering the family tree and bloodline.

Try to be in your parents' shoes for six decades and imagine how much you would treasure holding your grandkids in your lap. That is immeasurable joy, right?

Look closely at your aging parents because you are looking at your future reflection. Take pictures, develop them, and print a few to represent the best of the time capsule. Nothing beats printed pictures for quick access and family reminiscing. Enjoy the company of your parents now that you can. Tell them you love them. Spend time in your parents' crowded house when aunts, uncles, and cousins visit. Sleep anywhere you find space—even on the floor. That quality time will survive in their memories, and they can tell stories about the good old days.

Do you want to offend your parents? Be manipulative, theatrical, and overreactive. Always making mountains out of molehills and blowing smoke chokes you and depletes your parents' happiness. Your parents will have you to blame for their high blood pressure. You do not want that.

Be the David of your time and let the story of your phenomenal achievements precede you. Bounce back up one more time than you fall. Be a good example for your siblings; that is one of your parents' wishes. No parents are happy when their offspring fails in life.

Know your position in the family pecking order. If you are the firstborn, behave like the squad leader. Tolerate and welcome more people in your orbit, but be assertive.

If you are the last child, look up to your older siblings and plan to do better than those who came before you. Be the closest to your parents; they need you to help them transition into life with an empty nest.

Middle children tend to build bridges by solving puzzles and finding the missing links. They are the antidote to family feuds and help the family find unity. They are the kingmakers. Of course, each person must keep their dignity and avoid cultural faux pas.

Each of your siblings has a unique role to play in the family. The domino effect of siblings' conduct is most obvious in family relationships. One good turn will lead to another. Imagine a family reunion that all the siblings want to attend. A bad turn can lead to family disassociation and siblings hating each other, which can cascade to future generations. Each sibling must find their niche and their voice. They should love and encourage each other. To avoid a kingdom in chaos—where what belongs to everybody belongs to nobody—the family must have a de facto leader who espouses cooperation and unity. When done right, your parents will be happy and feel blessed that their legacy will live on when God calls them home. Life can be simple; you come into this world with nothing, and you leave with nothing.

You must play your part in your family. If you choose to go rogue and disrupt the family's pecking order, your family structure could crumble. You do not want that—unless you want your parents' curse.

You may pass up on your friends, but you may not pass up on or neglect your siblings. If you do that, your parents will take no pride in raising you. The tables will turn, and your parents will depend on you. Your parents growing old and becoming senior citizens beats the alternative of dying young. Recognize the urgency of the moment. Early and frank discussions about your parents' long-term care are important.

Talk and get your parents' insight on the best way to make them comfortable when the tide turn. Knowing their plans will go a long way in helping you help care for your aging parents.

Your parents may be experiencing muscle loss or other health ailments, but their ability to see bullshit remains sharp. Never disrespect their wishes. Your parents want to be around their lifelong friends; do not uproot them and deny them that social support system.

They probably prefer to maintain their living routines in areas they know and are familiar with. They are more trustful of the doctors who have seen them for most of their lives. As your parents age, they may cherish their immediate family and extended family more than ever. If possible, live close to your parents, move them close to you, or move them in with you. Consider all the options as you take care of your aging parents.

You may have to help your parents declutter and fix up house. They might need help paying their bills. Teach them how to use new technologies, particularly transaction alerts. Address the overwhelming effects of digital media on their lives. A discussion that must be had is scammers targeting the elderly with phone calls and emails.

Living to be an octogenarian or a centenarian is a blessing because many people kick the bucket much earlier. Treat your parents like you treasure the limited time you still have with them. Make them smile often. Make the times you spend with them memorable. Cultivate it now. Your parents will reciprocate by appreciating and loving you more. Those will be the sweet memories you will hold onto when they are gone.

CHAPTER 20

FAMILY MEMBERS

GG says we are all imperfect people. Nothing is perfect here on earth—not even you or your family. Do not allow stumbles to become tumbles. Each of us has different genetic markers that make us think and act differently. No family has a perfect relationship. Even among the twelve disciples, there was Judas.

Your family is not bad because the siblings sometimes have arguments. Do not forget the leap of faith that put your family where it is. There will be rivalries, money fights, sweat equity discussions, competitive spirits, and people feeling sidelined. Frankly, no one wants to be marginalized. Do you?

Be empathic. Avoid giving oxygen to any family strife. You have the choice to accept your family as is and look beyond those imperfections or be a lonely, miserable creature. Who wants to be a hermit?

If you could see yourself inside out, you would be amused, tongue-tied, and amazed by the bunkers you exhibit. Imagine what others see in you and their views about you.

By virtue of knowing no one is perfect, you can know what you are looking for before you start looking. Since you know what you are looking for, you will find it.

Accepting everyone as they are is necessary for seeing the good in others. Call upon your better angels when you deal with others. Build upon your common interests and then address any sticky situations. Get along as happily as possible. Ready, set, go. It is not unusual for brothers and sisters to rough up each other for one thing or another. The memories of younger ones fighting back, withstanding, and overcoming the older siblings' domination are etched into the deep experiences siblings share. With siblings, your relationship has been forged under extensive pressure.

Each of the siblings uniquely sees things from where they stand. A little competition and some bond building is all right. The Olympics speak to it. Sister countries compete for the pride of standing on the podium to receive a medal, particularly the gold, and listening to the National Anthem piercing a moment of silence. All families squabble and compete.

Although siblings may have the same mother and father, each one is blessed with different viewpoints, strengths, and weaknesses. One person may see the glass as half full, and the other describes it as half empty. Do not be surprised if one sibling feels the others are favored by their parents. Another may feel the others are just luckier for whatever is going on in their life. Sound familiar? There is always going to be some tug and pull in sibling relationships.

Although siblings each have their sins, there will be no hesitancy among them to cast the first stone. Try to see differences of opinion as input to help you manage your expectations.

Any good argument makes sense until you hear the other side. Adding salt to food enhances the flavor of the food, right?

If you add a grain too many, the food might be inedible. That's what happens when you try to outdo your siblings in arguments. One of the best ways to eliminate sibling differences is to respect one another. We all have ten fingers. The fingers are different sizes, and each of them plays a different role. It is the same for each member of your family. When you need a crazy person, send the crazy one. When you need the sweet-talker, send him. Can you imagine not having them and having to sacrifice the book-smart nerd who would be overwhelmed in areas where others can easily thrive?

Infighting is much more evident with grown-up siblings, spouses, and kids. Uncles, aunts, cousins, nephews, and nieces quarrel too. Your family is not the exception. What is different is how fast families reconcile and let bygones be bygones after heated exchanges. The families that get along know, despite their rivalries, they are a family. Of course, blood is thicker than water. Strangely, your siblings can telepathically feel when something has gone awry with a member of the family. They may check in on you because of a dream or just being concerned. Inclination confirmed!

Do not let sibling infighting water down that blood bond. You will be missing something if you emotionally detach yourself from your siblings. Because your siblings know you so well, they can read you inside out. Count on your siblings to watch out for your interests, particularly when you are on stage and blinded by the limelight. You may be on the way to burning up like a firework starburst. Someone has to tell you the emperor has no clothes. When the show ends, you will be thankful your behind was covered. Siblings are there to cover your behind.

You should rely on people who care about you to help you stay sane. You may feel some family members lifting you up and some tearing you down. Do not let anyone steal your joy. Be humble and tolerant as they file down some of your rough edges. Listen to the canary in the coal mine. Never take family criticism as the kiss of death.

Try to have each other's backs. Support each other. Be there for each other. Care for each other. Never be too busy for your family. Pull together and not apart. The sum is often greater than the parts. Make yourself an impactful family team member. Only a few burdens are heavy when everybody lifts because the burden is lighter. Have you heard the sound of one hand clapping? Appreciate your family's hands clapping together and working in tandem. You need to build inside-out friendships with your siblings. Everyone should value each other. Friendships with one another should be one of your family's greatest assets.

In family settings, there should be no winner or loser mindsets. Make no one feel like less. Leverage the privilege of teamwork and partnership. Allow each person to find their passion and voice.

Siblings who work together in engaging life obstacles are happier. Give your family the time they deserve—unless you want to be one of those people on their deathbeds who regret not being on amenable terms with their families. Now is your come-to-Jesus' moment. Love your siblings. Do not wait for the cock to crow thrice.

In life, you have the freedom to choose a lot of things—but not the freedom to choose your parents and siblings. That decision rests upon your parents' hands. Modern families may beg to differ since you can add adoptions and surrogate pregnancies to the mix.

Your brothers and sisters will be different in their own ways, but in some ways, you are all the same. You all will take after your parents in some form or another; whether you like it or not, you are united by your bloodline. You and your siblings are linked on a long chain. If you do not love your family, you cannot get your money back. Suck it up and adapt. Sibling relationship are like used cars that come as is. Do you want it to ride better? Fix it. Good or bad, make the best of the hand you are dealt.

Whether you are the eldest, in the middle of the birth order, or the last in the pack, respect each other equally. Respect begets respect. You are not the only grain of sand on the beach. Other grains of sand have their places on the beach too. In the sky, every star has a place. Each person is unique and rightfully here on Mother Earth for a purpose.

Each of your siblings is beautiful, depending on what you are looking for. If you can, help them prepare for their catwalk on the runway.

Put your ability to adjust and readjust as quickly as necessary on display by respecting that one man's meat is another man's poison. Be understanding and tolerate others' positions as much as possible.

Most of your early formative years were likely spent around your siblings, which will help breed love-hate relationships. Even if you are in a warm, loving home, life can throw curveballs at you. Bickering among family members is common. If you fight each other, learn to forgive and forget. If you hold grudges, a cancerous anger can wear down your soul.

If you bear grudges, you are fanning your own depression. The worst fruit of anger is revenge because it triggers an endless cycle of retaliation. No revenge is as sweet as forgiveness. Forgiveness heals wounds and gives you peace of mind.

You and your siblings are cut from one cloth; it is important to try to amend any brewing feuds. A dog does not bite its own tail. If you hurt your siblings, you are biting your own tail.

Loose lips sink ships. Letting your family's secrets out of the bag can be a good reason for hanging up phone. Nurture healthy relationship among yourselves. Try to enjoy your treasured bottle of wines with your siblings as you reminisce about the good old days, share your made-up war stories, and thump your chest.

Appreciate your siblings as they are. Be the peacemaker. Build bridges instead of walls. Everyone is entitled to their own opinion. Do not be a know-it-all. When issues come up, defuse them quickly. Compromise, laugh, be real, be there, and show up for each other.

Celebrate your brothers and sisters, enjoy them, let them enjoy your company, and be happy. Make the best of your bloodline. Let it be a showcase of love.

Do not let your siblings' anger simmer. Work inside out to help each other get unstuck. Your siblings' problems, in part, are yours too. Show empathy, resourcefulness, and kindness in finding answers. Be your siblings' biggest cheerleader.

It is not about finishing first. It is about working together to help each other thrive and successfully register a win on your life journey. Cherish your bloodline.

Be vigilant for dysfunctional dynamics of certain family members: the flamethrower, the troublemaker, the fearmonger, the drama queen, and the all-time attention seeker. If any of these characters are in your family, mentioning their names brings nothing but pain. They feel like an invisible albatross. Take heart because the crazy people in your life are there to help you balance your life.

People are neither completely round nor square. Do not discount them completely since even a broken clock is right twice daily. Value the dissenting voice of reason. Create goodwill to make them open up to you. You cannot come to the table with an attitude. If you do, you will not hear others—and others will not hear you. Everyone will be acting out their feelings. Do you want others to impose their attitudes on you?

Not all of your siblings are going to be like you. A few may see you as the big elephant in the room. Acknowledge the situation and ask for help in turning around their feelings. Watch your behavior toward them. In some cases, things are better not said to avoid stirring the hornets' nest. Your language drives others' behavior.

Pay attention to family members to your right and left. Nobody is a nobody. You may think you know them, but sometimes what they get into will bewilder even your parents. Yes, some people have some mystery about them. Accept your limitations in reading others' minds.

There are no excuses. You have the power to make your family members happy by entering or leaving the room. Figure out what the situation calls for and act accordingly.

It is hard to give what you do not have. Be happy yourself before trying to make others happy. Happiness is one of the many contagious moods you can display. Your siblings are likely to reciprocate the moods you exhibit.

If you are a jolly person, your siblings will see you as amiable. If you display a corrosive attitude, you will get harshness in return. If you vehemently reject oddities, they will abstain from such practices around you.

You do not have to possess everything to be happy, but you have to make the best of everything you have. Try to influence the family members around you. You will be remembered by the doors you opened or closed for their benefit.

Your siblings may want to do the right thing, but they might not know what that is. Show them what is right with your actions and by what you accept or reject. If you do, they will know where to look for the rising sun and the setting sun. Be as predictable as possible.

We are not living in a utopian world—expect family disagreements. Every sane person should be scared when their imperfection is under a glaring light. To preserve themselves, people may resort to offensive or defensive stances without considering how much they put off others. Try to abstain from seeing any family member as an existential threat. Even when you disagree with them, try to actively listen to their points of view. Where siblings stand determines where they sit. The way they see things depends on how things are inside them.

You have no one pointing a gun at your head to partake in the family feud. Pick your battles. Knowing when to leave the table is wisdom.

If you stand for what is right, even if you lose that argument, you will win when the truth is revealed.

Do not wait for a majority vote to lead. If you see a void, fill it, show enthusiasm and passion, and be a beacon of peace. Be a reference point for the rest.

If you run with the wolves, you will learn how to howl. With the hyenas, you will learn to eat nearly everything. When you fly with the golden eagles, you will soar to great heights. Eagles are tenacious, and they are not scavengers. Make a point to help your family get through the wilderness of life happily as they navigate their worldly challenges.

When opportunity allows, bring your siblings and their families together. Vacation together and party hard. Do not overlook geography and its impact on family dynamics. If possible, live closer. The more grown-up siblings and their families see each other, the stronger their relationships will be. Siblings living in different states or countries do not make it any easier. Sibling relationships diminish when they are not seeing each other for years. Love grows with proximity, and it tends to wane with distance and time.

Get to know each other more as grown siblings with wives and kids. Stop hating each other when you're alive and crying at death. That is hypocrisy. Accept each other now. Tolerate each other now. Live happily now.

Embrace opportunities that bring your family together to socialize and bond. Significant events in family members' lives offer great get-together opportunities: birthdays, anniversaries, graduations, weddings, new jobs, and promotion celebrations. Funerals, though somber moments, are another chance to reconnect with relatives. Do not forget to take advantage of special holidays for family get-togethers.

If possible, plan a yearly or biannual get-together at different family members' houses. Make the get-together a family tradition. Make it a memorable event for family members to look forward to. Welcome newcomers to the fold, reaffirm your family tree and oral histories, values, and identity, and party like the world is coming to an end. The commute, the reception, the party, and the socializing all create memories.

You may coordinate with other family members and take a vacation as a group to historic sites, beaches, or cities. When possible, consider day trips. There is nothing wrong with visiting and appreciating local attractions that out-of-states tourists flock to. They are often overlooked by local residents. Convince your family to visit a theme park. The trip will not be cheap, given amusement park ticket prices and hotel and food bills, but you will be mightily rewarded with first-class amusement and fun memories.

A trip to Walt Disney World, Universal Studios, or SeaWorld should be on your bucket list. Four nights and five days will do. Day 1 is arrival; days 2 and 3 are for outings, day 4 is for resting and socializing, and day 5 is departure. Cut the coat according to your size. Never overbook your days. A busy day will heighten stress levels and counter the essence of sharing quality time with loved ones.

A chunk of your vacation cost will go to the hotel room. If you do not plan to stay in the hotel room most of the day, and you are on a budget, why pay for a very expensive room when a less expensive one with most amenities will do? Paying for meals and drinks will get your attention quickly. Consider a hotel with free continental breakfasts.

The joy of a family vacation is more than staying in an expensive hotel. It is the sum of activities, meals, funny moments, and personal interactions. Witnessing the elation in the eyes of relatives enjoying each other's company is priceless. Make each facet of the vacation experience count.

It is great to pick up souvenirs to represent your vacations. As the years pass, those souvenirs will bring back memories of the good times you had. They will give you something to tell stories about. Delight others, reminisce, and smile. Looking back, it will all be worth it.

Take pictures and frame them for posterity.

Families taking vacation together tend to be closer than to those who allow the tyranny of distance and time to separate their family closeness. In close families, third cousins know their bloodline. In families lacking closeness, first cousins never know each other. What a shame that is!

If building family relationships is important to you, vacationing together will do it. Three family trips before a child leaves home will be ample to nourish good memories.

CHAPTER 21

END OF LIFE

GG says death is fact of life—and a tough topic to be had early. As much as it might hurt, talking about death should not be taboo.

You are going to die at some point. Death is part in the cycle of life. You have an appointed hour to meet your maker. What is not certain is when and how it will come. You only wish you knew. It is a suspended animation.

Live like you are going to die tomorrow and enjoy every moment. When possible, surround yourself with positive and cheerful people. It's easier to be happy with such a crowd. While planning for the future, enjoy the people around you.

Be kind to your family members and treat them as you would want to be treated. If you have always been nice to them, your guilt-free conscience will have no room for regrets in case of their sudden death.

The first dead body you see will be forever etched in your psyche. Don't worry. This is normal. Over time, you will see more death, and it will become a much more common phenomenon.

A discussion to have when you are healthy is what to do if you find yourself in a terminally ill vegetative state. Are you an advocate of tethering to dear life at all costs, dragging your family to hell and back, and spending the family fortune in futility? Why not permit yourself and your family to surrender your life when the commonsense threshold of living turns into hell for everyone? Consider having an advance directive in place.

Do your best every day—and be happy you have done all you can for that day. You have more priorities than you have time. Be ready to meet your destiny. No one lives forever, and the idea of being the first is an illusion. Funeral planning is another sore topic. It is good to know what to do before, during, and after funeral. Funding funeral expenses, choice of interment (burial or cremation), casket selection, cemetery, and processions are among things coming to bear soon after death. Discussing matters of this nature should be done earlier in life when you still have the capability and capacity to do so.

Unless you have money stashed away, not enough can be said about having funeral insurance. It will allow you to retain funeral home services. A one-stop shop that can handle the soup to nuts with your approval and lighten the burden your family will bear during the early days of bereavement.

The grieving process is like a roller coaster and a marathon. People grieve differently. Expect to grieve differently. If necessary, seek a grief counselor for help.

Your pain may be debilitating from the onset, but it should heal with time. Your pain may be episodic. You may witness delayed crying spells triggered by old memories. Whatever degree of hurt you experience, try to console yourself. Seek solace in God. Let your faith be your anchor. What is done is done. Do amends if so urged. Move on and live life in the best way you know how.

Hopefully, at the end of time, the dead and the living shall meet again.

As a young person, you may feel immortal, but the facts do not support immortal beings.

By midlife, your aches and pains will force you to accept that none of your body parts retain their youth. You will lose people you know. It will seem like when it rains, it pours. One bad turn triggers an avalanche of bad turns. Do not be taken aback when you experience many deaths of people you know and love in short order. It happens more often than you can imagine. A grandfather passes, and the grandmother passes just a handful of months or years later.

Among the close relatives you could lose are your grandparents, parents, uncles, and aunts. Siblings and cousins may make the count. Your own kids, nephews, and nieces are not excluded. It can happen to close friends, neighbors, coworkers, and members of your community. The worst would be you or your wife. Each death will affect you and your family dynamics.

Losing the people you care about is always painful. Take comfort in the belief that God giveth and God taketh.

Live each day honorably and like you know death may be at the door. Show people you love them. Tell people you love them. Be at peace with yourself and the people and things around you.

In life, you will run into many intersections. It is important to take the right exit. Get to your destination at the target hour. Do not let your lifestyle derail you. Set your compass, keep your eyes on it, and navigate to your objective.

Along the journey, pay attention to the people on your left and right. Communicate regularly with those transponders on your pathway and recalibrate regularly. Along the line, share your top priorities of the day. Learn, grow, adapt, and enjoy your purpose in life.

Never abandon your vision, your values, or others in your environment.

Life is like a staircase. Some people will be going up, and some will be coming down. Touch and positively impact the lives of others along your journey. Love your neighbor.

As you look back at the end of your life, you will not wish you were alone on a tropical island. You will savor your relationships with others. Cherish life's sweet moments when you physically and mentally can. If you are blessed to be a centenarian, you might be physically unable to enjoy things as your younger self did. Since life expectancies are many years less than one hundred, consider yourself lucky if you are among the few who become a centenarian. Live your life honorably and have a sense of purpose and a deserving urgency. Now is the time to correct your life trajectory for good. Hail the adventure of life. Bask in the sun now. Leave your mark on the world now. Today, you have options, but tomorrow, you might not. Tomorrow may not come if today turns out to be anything but normal. Today could be your last day alive.

PART V

AT FORTY, TIGER LOOKS BACK

Two scores had passed since GG put *Father's Gift* in Tiger's hands. Tony, one of his few childhood friends, said, "He had it made." "Not so fast," Tiger responded. "It took a lot of individual effort and time to acquire knowledge. It required even more determination to practice the knowledge and produce results. There is pressure to win—and a lot more pressure not to lose."

The discussion sent Tiger deep down memory lane. Tiger thought about what could have been and what is. Tony heard Tiger like he never had before and had an epiphany: "Pass it on."

CHAPTER 22

TIGER AT IT

According to Tiger, without the nuggets of wisdom sprinkled at various stages of life in GG's road map, *Father's Gift*, he would have stumbled cluelessly through life's darkness. *Father's Gift* enabled Tiger to take a peek into the future and see the key things at each corner through the prism of time and space.

A few things flashed in the back of Tiger's mind. His life's path was in contrast to the paths taken by Blake, a school buddy, and Bradley, a college classmate. His other tugging memory was about his family relationships.

GG's tips helped Tiger manage life situations. Even when Tiger failed, he learned more from his mistakes than from others' failures. He rebounded quickly.

What happened and what happens afterward matter. Things behind and things before matter. Where and when you are present or absent matter. Knowing when to learn and when to perform matter too. Tiger knew those lessons. Tiger believed he was saved by the bell: *Father's Gift*.

Tiger thought about Blake. Tiger had been naturally attracted to the hippie boy's persona. In this particular situation, Tiger was able to catch himself before he fell off the cliff. Blake would have fed Tiger his Kool-Aid.

Tiger did some experimenting in things he was not supposed to be doing, but luckily, his guilty conscience got the best of him. Before long, he ceased and desisted, saved his honor, and held onto the pride GG had in him.

In high school, Blake was the man. He was handsome, athletic, and tall. He was a smooth talker and a street kingpin with plenty of cash to spare, which made him a girl magnet. Blake smoked and drank even though he was not twenty-one. Blake was from a well-to-do family. Other than his academic weakness, Blake had it all.

Blake's street activities got him entangled with the law just days before his high school graduation. Blake did three years in prison for selling drugs. As if that was not bad enough, the two mothers of the babies Blake had out of wedlock in his last year in high school took him to court for child support soon after his release from prison.

Blake's family disowned him and turned their backs on him for bringing shame to the family's name. Blake, born with silver spoon in his mouth, had lost his way in life.

With Blake's prison record, finding a decent job was difficult. Many prospective employers looked at former inmates as criminals, which was not true. Recidivism continues to negatively affect those who have done their time and repented.

Finding a job was difficult for Blake—and so was keeping any job he found.

Blake took on drinking to numb his disappointments in life. His efforts to tame his demons by checking into alcohol and drug treatment facilities were fruitless.

Blake had fallen from the most popular guy in high school to being homeless within a decade.

According to Tiger, he would have been Blake without *Father's Gift* tethering him to the moral high ground. The book helped him navigate life's minefields, realize and hone his endowed gifts, become a man with constitution and solid character, and abstain from violating the law.

Tiger then thought about Bradley.

Although Tiger came from a family with humble beginnings, he attended an Ivy League school. Were it not for his full academic scholarship, his parents' income would not have been enough to pay half the cost of a semester, board, and other expenses.

Tiger knew his ticket to higher education had to be self-made. He studied with a passion and sought assistance from anybody who would help him.

Bradley used to call Tiger a book worm, but Tiger was unfazed.

Tiger's laser-like focus on education shortchanged his social grace—and it was unvarnished. Tiger accepted the trade-off until he completed college and landed the job of his dreams.

In short order, Tiger blossomed. He applied the lessons learned from *Father's Gift*. Tiger is a great team player, a great follower, and a great leader. His leadership and public speaking skills always shine like the North Star.

For Tiger, every challenge was a mission and an opportunity to earn his stripes. Like a guided rocket, Tiger moved from launching pad to his target. He earned a reputation for achieving results and making a positive impact. His employer rewarded him with increased responsibilities and handsome pay packages.

Tiger worked his way up the management ladder. His hourly pay exceeded six times the federal minimum hourly wage by his early thirties. From *Father's Gift*, his internalized lessons of what you make does not count as much as what you save and invest in preparation for the rainy days was alive and awake. Tiger was good at money management.

Bradley, the college classmate, is a financial market trader and earns a lot more than Tiger does. However, he is in over his head with debt. Tiger feels proud of his well-managed lifestyle.

Bradley bought one of the best houses in his affluent suburban neighborhood and leased upscale cars every year. Bradley's wild and lavish lifestyle was evident in his designer clothes, late-night parties, gambling, and vacations. Bradley had a carefree life and lived it to the fullest. However, his peace of mind was questionable given his worries about paying his overdue bills.

Tiger bought a starter house, which was convenient for his commute, and he kept his cars for six years before heading to the dealership for a replacement vehicle. Tiger knew the best new cars make the best used cars—and they get the best resale value. Tiger's vehicle upgrade was based on value added and practical utility as espoused in *Father's Gift*.

Living a modest and judicious live and investing his savings diligently resulted in Tiger amassing his dream net worth—more than twelve times his annual income—much earlier than he had planned.

What a difference between them! Bradley has financial woes, and Tiger is financially secured.

◆ ◆ ◆

Among Tiger's family vacations, the one that stood out more than others was the four-day trip to Resort at the Lake.

The whole family was there. GG (Grandpa George) and Gma (Grandma Anna) were there. Uncle Monty and Auntie Rita were there. Auntie Viola was there. Auntie Rita's son, Hawk came too. Mom Jena and Daddy Johnny brought Charlie (Tiger's younger brother) and Eva (Tiger's younger sister) along with them. Tiger arrived with his wife, Angela, and his son, Tom.

That vacation was the only one they had with four generations of Tiger's family. It was the one when GG crowned Uncle Monty the BBQ king. Monty took pride in being the family's master chef. He bragged about his secret sauces and marinated his pork ribs with special sauce. The ribs were juicy and tender, and the meat fell easily off the bone. Monty shared the secret sauce ingredients with Tiger, his favorite nephew.

Hawk, Charlie, and Tiger spent hours riding the dirt bikes they rented from the resort. The fun lasted until Hawk drove off trail and crashed into the woods. Hawk got up with more than his bruised ego. His right forearms sustained several abrasions.

Auntie Rita blamed Tiger for coming up with the dirt bike idea. Tiger felt hurt and wondered why Auntie Rita was always on his case. Mom Jena came to the defense of her son, stating that her older sister was jealous of her and her family. To deescalate the situation, GG barked, "Y'all cut it out and stop being childish." They did.

After a few minutes, Mom Jena and Auntie Rita went back to their usual yapping and laughing like nothing had happened. Tiger witnessed a sisterly squabble that would not run deep. Family may be at odds with each other, but they should make up quickly. A few minutes later, Hawk and Tiger had a double chest bump. That was family love.

Tiger's family did some trout and bass fishing, and Auntie Rita caught more fish than anyone else. In jest, GG took credit for teaching her how to fish, but he did not take the blame for Mom Jena not catching even a minnow.

At the resort's entertainment building, there were game room, slot machines, a bingo room, and a karaoke section. Family members milled from one room to another, depending on their interest. Eva hit the jackpot, and the slot machine sounded like a broken record player as it spewed out five hundred dollars in coins.

Auntie Viola was definitely the best in karaoke.

Tiger's family rented two-person pedaling canoes. Everyone wore safety vests because the resort required guests to so. In pairs, they jumped into the canoes. They raced around the lake. On the timed canoe race, to everyone's surprise, Charlie's canoe posted the fastest time, which earned him a yellow bandana. He proudly wore it around his left hand as the champ.

Tiger's family ended that day at the high-rise water splash. It was memorable watching the family laughing deliriously as they cascaded and tumbled down the water slide. Gma gave GG a sudden nudge, pushing him off the water slide unexpectedly, which was a sight to see. Tiger had never seen GG and Gma as excited as on the fun ride.

Later that day, the family watched a movie in the theater.

On the last day, the family gathered at the freshly cut lawn by the lake and watched the beautiful sunset. Gma told folk stories that her own mama had shared with her about eighty-five years ago. GG and Gma repeated some of their favorite stories with a touch of wisdom acquired along the way. They urged the family to continue to love each other, help and care for one another, and treat each other kindly. Gma asked them to hold hands while she led a prayer. Immediately afterward, GG and Gma received hugs from each of them before dismissing them for the night.

Angela, Tiger's wife, was very happy to partake in the family reunion because her family never had such a get-together. Tiger swore to carry on the family tradition.

That was the last vacation GG and Gma had with the entire family before they both passed. GG passed and Gma passed from a broken heart a week before the one-year anniversary.

Tiger's family took consolation in GG saying, "Your life is like a hired taxi. The meter keeps ticking, moving, or standing, and you must pay your fare at your drop-off point." GG and Gma had reached their drop-off station and paid their fares.

Tiger knew his success and happiness had not come by accident. He was not inoculated from the ups and downs of his life journey. Very early, Tiger knew life was a stage—and actions and reactions have real consequences. He could thrive or languish; it was choice. Of course, Tiger chose to thrive.

Living in an underserved zip code, it did not take Tiger long to figure out that some folks had it made, and others did not. Many of the neighborhood kids had hoped for better lives that never came.

Tiger did not just accept being born into humble beginnings; he embraced it and believed he was destined to be well-to-do. Tiger's quest and pursuit of excellence led him to find his groove, live a balanced-sweet life, and inspire teachable moments, particularly for his best friend.

At forty years of age, the good life certainly adorns Tiger. Relationships worth envying exist in every aspect of his life. His wife, Angela, and son, Tom, were his bedrock. With the early grooming Tom was getting, Tiger could see his son becoming a politician someday. Thanks for *Father's Gift* and Angela doing everything right, Tiger's vocation has been very rewarding and fulfilling. Tiger maintained very warm relationships with his extended family. He was a happy man, and he was at peace with himself because he knew GG would be very proud of the man he turned out to be.

Tiger's family and friends always gave him home-team cheers, and they meant everything to him.

Tiger looked forever young because of the healthy habits he cultivated and maintained. Tiger laughed at a pin drop, lived each day with purpose, and treated others with kindness. He trusted God to bear his worries. He felt spiritually connected to God. Tiger was mostly at ease with himself.

Why reinvent the wheel? Time passes, and some things change, but other things remain constant. A head start in your life journey is good, and Tiger is happy to welcome anyone to the *Father's Gift* conversation.

CHAPTER 23

PASS IT ON

Tiger's reflections on his life provided his best buddy, Tony, the mirror he critically needed to look at himself, see himself, and judge himself. Tiger's words sparked something anew in Tony and awoke a sense of self-awareness that would have been, in the past, foreign to him. It was the first time Tony had such epiphany.

Immediately, Tony knew his family needed a course correction. Tony's family relationship was at the opposite end of the spectrum compared to Tiger's family's sense of closeness and oneness.

Although Tony's family resided in reasonably close proximity, in the state of their birth, they lacked cohesion and love. Tony's family held grudges, and their jealousy transcended normal family dynamics.

Tony was seen as standoffish by his siblings.

It was a surprise when Tony called for the family to have a reunion at Cruise Ultimate. Tony wanted his four siblings and their families to gather together in close quarters, hash out their issues, bury the hatchet, and rekindle and reconnect their brotherly love.

Tony's family took him up on the call for the cruise, showed up, and showed out. Tony took a leadership role. He took pages from *Father's Gift* and marinated his family with stories for a rebirth.

Tony's family was very receptive to *Father's Gift* and learning about self-empowerment, building wealth, and family relationships. It opened their eyes to see their character flaws and the need for a rebirth.

Tony promised each person a copy of *Father's Gift*. They were all delighted, particularly Tony's youngest sister, Tina, who jokingly said she wished she had read the book in her formative days. She would have picked a better husband. Everybody laughed.

They wasted more time talking about the weather before moving on to the important things. The pleasantries were over, and official business of the health of Tony's family relationship took center stage. That was settled as the family started enjoying the seven-day cruise.

They had fun. They enjoyed the ocean liner's opulent offerings and all-you-can-eat gourmet foods and drinks. The game room, casino and dance hall were open twenty-four-seven. Most of the cruise guests appeared to be on cloud nine.

Each day, the ship went from one historical landmark to another. And each day greeted them with different vibes.

The gorgeous coastline and wonderful secluded beaches were inviting. Tony and his family feasted their eyes on the majestic views and wild creatures. Watching the dolphins gracefully playing next to the ship topped the chart.

The butterfly sanctuary was a sight to see. The visit to the historic enclave was worthy of every minute spent there.

The cruise stopped at several islands for souvenirs and pictures. At a few locations, they tasted authentic local cuisine. The cultural attractions were a great treat. Cruise Ultimate was rejuvenating for all. Everyone was happy and had euphoric feelings of the cruise never coming to an end. At the port, Tony and his family came together for group hug. There were hugs after hugs with each other. Tony's family agreed, moving forward, to make up for the lost time in their family relationships and do better. They left behind the nemesis they brought with them at sea and took their joyous hearts home. Reinforcing your family relationships and history can begin with you.

Yes, *Father's Gift* is reaching more people!

The knowledge shared here may be taken for granted if you already know it, but what about the many others who need to know? Yes, a faraway place is close for some people, but what about those who are coming from afar? Some people live faraway—and you may be among them. With *Father's Gift*, you will not make the mistake of going on life's journey blindfolded.